Favorite Comfort Food

THE BEST OF MARTHA STEWART LIVING

Favorite Comfort Food

A Satisfying Collection of Home Cooking Classics

Copyright © 1999
Martha Stewart Living
Omnimedia LLC
20 West 43rd Street,
New York, NY 10036

Originally published in book form by
Martha Stewart Living Omnimedia LLC
in 1999. Published simultaneously
by Clarkson N. Potter, Inc.,
Oxmoor House, Inc., and Leisure Arts.

A portion of this work
was previously published in
MARTHA STEWART LIVING.

Manufactured in the
United States of America.

Library of Congress Cataloging
in Publication Data is available
upon request.
ISBN 0-8487-1898-4 (hardcover)
0-8487-1899-2 (paperback)
item #109133

Executive Editor: Kathleen Hackett
Art Director: Linda Kocur
Text: David Nussbaum
Assistant Art Director: Jill Groeber

contents

Introduction 9

Long Mornings

Home for Lunch

What to Have for Dinner

"My very favorite thing to eat is white bread with big fat slices of tomatoes and that sandwich spread…you know, the kind with the relish in it."

"…raisin bran with skim milk late at night…"

"…ice-cold condensed milk…I've been known to eat it straight from the can…with a spoon. I don't buy it anymore, because I can't stop eating it."

"…my garden cucumbers, sliced crosswise and drizzled with honey from my bees…"

"…all kinds of potpies, especially rabbit potpies…"

"…pierogies…cabbage pierogies cooked in a hot pan with a little brown butter…I can eat at least twenty of them."

"…white bread with lots of butter…"

"…my mother's black-bottom pie…"

"Anything Alexis makes is delicious, especially her coconut cake. She stacks it a mile high and hand-grates the coconut."

Martha Stewart

long mornings

chapter one

Even in the busiest lives there are days when we must slow down.

The flavors of morning are pure and simple. Slices of perfectly ripe muskmelon—so juicy, aromatic, and silky textured—are a prelude to thick slabs of toast and sweet homemade preserves. The aroma of freshly ground, hand-brewed coffee beckons. But all this is just the beginning—there's a griddle heating in the kitchen, pancake batter being whisked, and bacon sizzling in a skillet.

There are times when we find time to sit for a few moments in a sunlit room, marveling at the comforting quiet of home. These are the mornings we can open the fridge and pantry doors, grab eggs and milk, oatmeal and honey. Rummage in the cupboards and the drawers for pans and bowls, whisks, spoons, and spatulas—and make a bit of joyful noise in the kitchen. This is the music of a real breakfast: kettle whistling; eggs cracking; pancake batter being whisked and hissing as it hits the hot griddle.

Though we know the tastes so well, favorite breakfasts never lose their power to please: a heaping bowl of oatmeal, plain or with loads of brown sugar; a creamy scramble of as many eggs as you want; or a mile-high stack of blueberry pancakes, drenched in maple syrup and melting butter, can always tempt us from a soft bed and sweet dreams. Most of the recipes in this chapter can be made in just a matter of minutes, not hours. Let the time that you save in the kitchen become yours to savor at the table. Delicious as our homemade French doughnuts are, don't devour them in two bites. Savor each luscious crumb. Take your time.

A bowl of thick Irish oatmeal
and a pot of breakfast tea provide
a warm beginning to the day.
Whether softened overnight or
slowly cooked that morning, the
steel-cut nuggets of whole grain
develop a nutty flavor and texture
like no other oatmeal. Add spoon-
fuls of brown sugar and splashes
of warm milk to make the cereal
as smooth and sweet as you like.

Oatmeal Four Ways

There are four ways to cook steel-cut oats (Irish or Scottish oatmeal) and good old-fashioned rolled oats; each yields a slightly different result. Traditionally, steel-cut oats are soaked overnight and quickly cooked the next morning. If you forget to soak them, just cook them longer. Toasting the oats adds a smoky flavor; boiling oatmeal until it is just firm (see Doug's Al Dente Oatmeal) makes it flakier. Serve with the selection of hot-cereal toppings on page 15.

Soaked Steel-cut Oats   makes 3¼ cups

Pinch of coarse salt
1 cup Irish, Scottish, or any
   steel-cut oatmeal

1. Bring 4 cups water and the salt to a boil in a medium saucepan. Turn off heat, stir in the oatmeal, cover, and let stand overnight (photo 1).

2. Place soaked oatmeal on medium-low heat, and cook, stirring occasionally until hot and creamy, 8 to 10 minutes. Serve hot with the toppings of your choice.

Unsoaked Steel-cut Oats   makes 3¼ cups

Pinch of coarse salt
1 cup Irish, Scottish, or any
   steel-cut oatmeal

Bring 4 cups water and the salt to a boil in a medium saucepan. Stir in oatmeal (photo 2). Reduce to a simmer; let cook, stirring occasionally, until oatmeal is tender but still retains some bite, about 30 minutes. Serve hot with the toppings of your choice.

Doug's Al Dente Oatmeal   makes 4 cups

Pinch of coarse salt
2½ cups old-fashioned rolled oats

Bring a large saucepan of water and the salt to a boil. Stir in the oatmeal, lower heat to medium, and cook, stirring occasionally, until al dente, about 7 minutes. Strain immediately under very hot water to rinse away excess starch (photo 3). Serve hot with the toppings of your choice.

Toasted Oatmeal   makes 4 cups

1 tablespoon unsalted butter
1 cup Irish, Scottish, or any
   steel-cut oatmeal, or 2½ cups
   old-fashioned rolled oats
   Pinch of coarse salt

Melt butter in a large heavy saucepan over medium heat. Add the oatmeal, and toast, tossing and turning the oats, until the oatmeal is browned and fragrant, about 4 minutes (photo 4). Add 4 cups water and the salt, and bring to a boil. Reduce to a simmer, cover, and cook until most of water has evaporated and the oatmeal is tender, about 30 minutes for the Irish oatmeal and 10 minutes for the old-fashioned rolled oats. Serve hot with the toppings of your choice.

The distinctive, hearty flavors of cracked wheat, soy flakes, and kasha (roasted buckwheat) blend in a bowl of our multi-grain cereal (right). Gentle simmering in apple juice makes the grains glisten; more natural sweetness comes from a topping of sautéed cranberries and oranges. A bowl of hot cereal becomes breakfast when something sweet and warm is spooned on top. Choose from among (below, clockwise from top left) golden wedges of pears softened in butter and sugar; a flecked-ivory vanilla cream; stewed apricots, prunes, and golden raisins; an amber pool of honey spiced with cinnamon and star anise; a crimson and gold compote of cranberries and oranges; a toasty granola mix with pecans; your favorite brown sugar; or toasted hazelnuts.

Multigrain Hot Cereal With Cranberries and Oranges

1   cup cranberries (fresh
     or frozen)
2   oranges, peeled and segmented
2   cups apple juice
1   cup cracked wheat
½   cup soy flakes
½   cup buckwheat kasha
¼   cup toasted hazelnuts

Any grain flakes may be used in place of the soy flakes.   **makes 4½ cups**

1. Heat a medium skillet over medium-high heat. Add cranberries and 2 tablespoons water. Cook until cranberries soften and release their juices, about 2 minutes. Stir in orange segments. Remove from heat, and set aside.

2. Bring apple juice and 3 cups water to a boil in a large saucepan. Add cracked wheat, reduce to a simmer, cover, and cook for 15 minutes. Add soy flakes, and cook, covered, 5 minutes more. Add kasha, and cook, covered, 10 minutes more. Uncover, and cook 5 minutes to let excess liquid evaporate. Spoon into individual bowls. Add the hazelnuts, and spoon fruit on top. Serve hot.

Hot-Cereal Toppings

Stewed Fruit   makes 1 cup

¼   cup brandy
1   vanilla bean, split and scraped
8   pitted prunes
12 dried apricot halves
¼   cup golden raisins

Place brandy, vanilla bean and pod, prunes, apricots, and raisins in a small saucepan with 2 cups water. Bring to a boil, reduce to a simmer, and let fruit cook until liquid is reduced by three-quarters. Serve warm over hot cereal. Rewarm stewed fruits as needed in a small saucepan over low heat.

Infused Honey   makes 1 cup

1   cup honey
4   star anise
4   cinnamon sticks

Warm all ingredients in a small saucepan over medium-low heat for 5 to 10 minutes. Turn off heat, and let rest for at least 30 minutes or overnight. Honey may be made and kept, up to 10 days, in an airtight container.

Sautéed Pears   serves 4

2   pears, peeled and cored
     Juice of 1 lemon
1   tablespoon unsalted butter
2   tablespoons sugar

Cut each pear into 8 wedges. Toss the pears and lemon juice in a medium bowl, and set aside. Melt the butter in a large skillet over medium heat. Add pears and ½ cup water. Sprinkle with the sugar. Simmer until water has evaporated and pears are golden brown, stirring occasionally, about 8 minutes. Serve warm.

Vanilla Cream   makes 2 cups

2   cups heavy cream
1   vanilla bean, split and scraped

Heat the cream and vanilla bean, with scrapings, in a small saucepan over very low heat until cream is just bubbling. Remove from heat; steep for about 20 minutes. Remove the bean before serving.

Toasted Granola   makes 1 pound

1   cup rolled oats
1   cup soy flakes
1   cup wheat flakes
½   cup packed light-brown sugar
1   cup roughly chopped pecans
     Zest of 1 orange
½   teaspoon freshly grated nutmeg
¼   teaspoon ground cinnamon
½   cup (1 stick) unsalted butter
¼   cup honey

Heat the oven to 350°. Combine the oats, flakes, brown sugar, pecans, orange zest, nutmeg, and cinnamon in a large bowl. Melt the butter and honey together in a small saucepan, and stir into oat mixture. Spread out onto a 7-by-11-inch baking pan, and bake until just golden brown, about 10 minutes. Let cool in pan. Mixture will harden as it cools. Break into pieces, and serve. Store in an airtight container up to 10 days.

Golden Porridge With Currant Cranberry Crust

2 tablespoons dried currants
2 tablespoons dried cranberries
2 tablespoons almond slivers
1 tablespoon plus 1 teaspoon sugar
2 tablespoons millet
1 large egg white
3/4 cup wheat berries
1/2 teaspoon salt
1 cup Irish oatmeal
1/2 cup milk
3 tablespoons molasses
3 tablespoons honey
3/4 teaspoon ground cinnamon

The crisp topping can be made ahead and kept in an airtight container for up to one week.   **serves 4**

1. Heat oven to 350°. Line an 11-by-17-inch baking sheet with parchment paper. In a small bowl, combine currants, cranberries, almonds, sugar, and millet. In another small bowl, whisk the egg white until it holds soft peaks. Add 1 tablespoon of egg white to dry mixture, and stir until coated. Discard any remaining egg white. Spread mixture on prepared baking sheet, and bake until almonds are golden, about 10 minutes. Remove from oven, and place on a rack to cool; set topping aside.

2. Fill a large pot with water; cover, and bring to a boil. Add wheat berries, and return to a boil. Cook until grains are al dente, about 30 minutes. Drain.

3. Meanwhile, bring 4 cups of water to boil in a medium saucepan. Add salt and oatmeal, and cook, stirring, until it begins to thicken, about 3 minutes. Reduce heat to medium low, and simmer until almost all the liquid is absorbed, about 30 minutes. Add the milk, molasses, honey, cinnamon, and cooked wheat berries, and cook, stirring constantly, until heated through and thick, about 5 minutes. Serve hot, sprinkled with reserved topping.

Oat Scones

1 1/4 cups whole-wheat flour
2 cups all-purpose flour
3/4 cup plus 1 tablespoon sugar
3/4 teaspoon salt
1 teaspoon baking soda
2 1/2 teaspoons baking powder
2 1/2 cups old-fashioned rolled oats
1 cup fresh sour cherries, roughly chopped
1 cup plus 2 tablespoons (2 1/4 sticks) chilled unsalted butter, cut into 1/2-inch pieces
2/3 cup buttermilk
1 tablespoon heavy cream

Sour cherries make delicious scones, but their season is short; as an alternative you can use blueberries, dried cherries or cranberries, or even raisins. Freezing the dough for at least a few hours before baking keeps the scones from spreading too much. The dough will keep in the freezer up to three weeks.   **makes 10**

1. Line an 11-by-17-inch baking sheet with parchment paper. Combine all the dry ingredients, reserving 1 tablespoon sugar, with the cherries in the bowl of an electric mixer fitted with the paddle attachment. Add butter, and mix on medium-low speed until the mixture resembles coarse meal. Add buttermilk, and mix until just combined.

2. Turn out the mixture onto a clean work surface. With hands, quickly pat mixture into a 16-by-3 1/2-inch rectangle. Score rectangle into ten triangles. Cover with plastic wrap, and transfer to the freezer for at least 2 hours.

3. Heat oven to 350°. Remove scored dough from the freezer, and cut into triangles with a sharp knife. Place scones 2 inches apart on the prepared baking sheet. Brush scones with heavy cream, and sprinkle with the reserved sugar. Bake until lightly golden, about 30 minutes; serve warm.

"It took me years to figure out how to make porridge like my Mom's—lumpy with brown sugar and butter. I pretend I'm getting four kids ready for school and making breakfast at the same time." —PETER MARS, ASSOCIATE STYLE EDITOR

A tray of traditional whole-grain breakfast favorites—slow-cooked porridge and oat scones—can take the chill off the coldest winter morning. Serve the steaming porridge in a café-au-lait bowl, sprinkled with a crunchy mix of almonds and dried fruits. Swaddle scones studded with tart cherries and lightly glazed with cream and sugar in a linen napkin—they are at their best still warm from the oven.

Coddled Eggs

Unsalted butter for greasing
2 teaspoons heavy cream
4 large eggs
Salt and freshly ground pepper

Coddling is a gentle steaming method that yields a tender egg. The eggs are cooked individually in coddling cups—ceramic cups with screw-on lids available in kitchen-supply stores. Four-ounce baby-food jars can be used as well. Delicious prepared with heavy cream and a light seasoning of salt and pepper, coddled eggs are particularly appealing when garnished with chopped herbs, onion, or cooked bacon.   **makes 4**

1. Line the bottom of a saucepan with a kitchen towel. Fill the pan with enough water to come just below the rim of the coddlers. Place over medium-high heat. Bring to a boil.

2. Butter the insides of each coddler. Pour $1/2$ teaspoon heavy cream in each. Add one egg; season with salt and pepper. Screw on lids tightly. Carefully place egg coddlers into boiling water.

3. Reduce heat to medium, and simmer for 4 minutes. Turn off heat, cover pan, and let stand for 6 to 7 minutes. Remove coddlers from water, unscrew lids, and serve immediately.

Scrambled Eggs

4 large eggs
Salt and freshly ground pepper
2 teaspoons unsalted butter

Nearly everyone has a preferred method for scrambling eggs; our favorite is the simplest of all—with no added milk or water, seasoned with only salt and pepper, and cooked in butter. The key is to beat the eggs briskly, incorporating air to produce large, fluffy curds.   **serves 2**

1. Combine the eggs with salt and pepper in a medium bowl, and whisk vigorously for 15 seconds. Melt the butter in a 7-inch nonstick skillet over medium-high heat.

2. When butter is melted and foamy, add the eggs. Reduce heat to medium. Using a rubber spatula or a flat wooden spoon, push eggs toward center while tilting skillet to distribute runny parts.

3. When eggs are almost set, scramble them some more, gently turning them over several times. Remove skillet from heat. Serve immediately.

Is there a more American way to start the day? Creamy scrambled eggs, crisp lean bacon, and buttered toast fill a sturdy white restaurant plate in generous portions, just as they would be served at the diner. With a glass of fresh squeezed orange juice and a bottomless cup of good coffee, there's no better fuel for the road.

A porcelain coddler is both a convenient cooking vessel and a charming way to serve a coddled egg. With a just-firm white and a thick flowing yolk, this most delicate of eggs should be eaten right from the cup, with a spoon. Or scoop it out with buttered toast fingers to soak up every morsel of delicious egg and the cream it is cooked in.

How to Make an Omelet

You need only an ovenproof nonstick skillet, a wire whisk, and a heat-resistant rubber spatula to make a perfect omelet. Fresh eggs, butter, salt, and freshly ground pepper will guarantee that your omelet tastes delicious. The best butter to use is clarified butter, which does not burn as easily as salted or unsalted butter. If you use regular butter, watch carefully to keep it from burning. Clarified butter is easiest to make in large quantities, and because it has no milk solids, which cause butter to turn rancid, it can be refrigerated for several weeks or frozen until needed. To clarify butter, cut a pound of unsalted butter into tablespoon-size pieces, and place in a small, deep saucepan. Melt the butter very slowly over low heat. The water in the butter will evaporate, and the milk solids will sink to the bottom of the saucepan. Skim off the foam that rises to the surface, and pour the clear, yellow melted butter off the milk solids at the bottom of the saucepan and into a glass jar; discard milk solids.

1. An omelet pan needs to be hot but not scalding. Heat 1 tablespoon clarified butter in a 10-inch skillet over medium-high heat. Place your hand above the skillet. When your palm feels warm, the skillet is ready to start cooking.

2. Whisk together 3 large eggs and salt and freshly ground pepper to taste while the pan is heating, not before. If they have to sit and wait for the pan, the whisked eggs will deflate. You want to incorporate lots of air into the mixture so that your omelet is light and fluffy. Drop a little whisked egg into the pan. If the egg sizzles and begins to fry, the pan is too hot.

3. Working quickly, pour the whisked eggs into the hot skillet. Reduce heat to medium. If you want to serve several omelets at once, turn the oven to low heat, about 200°, and place the serving plates in it.

4. Simultaneously whisk the eggs and shake the skillet vigorously back and forth over heat for less than a minute. You want to keep the eggs moving, incorporating some of the runny parts with the more-cooked parts until there are some curds swimming in the eggs. Stop whisking. The key to producing an omelet with a fluffy, very smooth surface is to stop whisking just before the egg sets.

Omelet making is a bit of morning magic. With a deft twist of the wrist, a shake, a fold and a flip, and a nonstick pan, turn three eggs into an elegant breakfast.

5. Continue cooking, making sure eggs cover the entire surface of the skillet. Using a rubber spatula, spread the runny egg out to the edges of the pan and over any holes that may have formed on the surface of the omelet.

6. With the handle of the pan pointing directly out toward you, sprinkle ½ cup of your favorite filling (see filling suggestions, page 22) over the left side of the eggs, leaving a small rim of egg around the edge. Run the rubber spatula along the right side of the omelet to loosen eggs from the skillet. Place the spatula under the right side of the eggs, making sure that the spatula is well underneath the eggs to offer maximum support, and lift the right side over the left in one fluid motion.

7. The folded omelet should look like a half moon. Lightly press down on the omelet with the spatula to seal the omelet together. Do not press hard; you do not want to flatten the curds. Check to make sure the handle of the skillet is still facing directly out toward you. Lift the skillet with one hand, and hold the plate with your other hand. Tilt the skillet, and let the curved edge of the omelet slide onto the plate. Quickly invert the skillet, folding the portion of the omelet that is left in the skillet over the curved edge already on the plate. Keeping the skillet at about stomach level with the handle facing directly out should help you do this.

8. Traditionally, omelets are garnished with something that relates to the filling, but this does not need to be a hard-and-fast rule. A simple sprig of parsley is sufficient. A garnish that's been strategically placed can also help mask an imperfection.

Martha's Soft-Boiled Eggs

4 large eggs
Coarse salt and freshly
ground pepper

Martha prefers coarse salt on her soft-boiled eggs, but use whatever salt you like best. Despite its name, the boiled egg shouldn't be boiled throughout the cooking process—a method that yields a rubbery result—but rather brought to a boil and then immediately removed from heat. Serve with buttered toast.   **serves 2**

Place the eggs in a saucepan large enough to accommodate them in a single layer. Fill the pan with cold water, covering the eggs by an inch. Set over medium-high heat, and bring to a boil. Turn off heat, cover, and let stand 1½ to 2 minutes. Remove eggs from the water. Serve immediately in egg cups—perfect for cracking and scooping the egg right from the shell. Season with salt and pepper.

Poached Eggs With Smoked Ham

1 tablespoon distilled white vinegar
4 large eggs
2 English muffins, cut in half
   crosswise
   Unsalted butter, for spreading
4 slices smoked or baked ham
   (about 4 ounces total)
   Salt and freshly ground pepper

A flawless poached egg is compact, with glistening whites clinging to a barely set yolk. Use the freshest eggs you can find: The thick albumen will hold its shape better around the yolk than that of older eggs.   **serves 4**

1. Set a rack in the top third of the oven, and heat the broiler. Fill a large, wide saucepan halfway with water, and bring to a boil over high heat. Reduce heat to medium, so that the water is just simmering, and add the vinegar.

2. Break 1 egg at a time into a small heat-proof bowl, about the size of 1 egg. Slightly immerse the bowl in the simmering water, and quickly slide in the egg. After all the eggs have been added, turn off the heat, cover the saucepan, and let stand for 2 to 3 minutes.

3. Meanwhile, toast the English muffins: Set them on a cookie sheet under the broiler, and toast until light golden brown on each side, about 1½ minutes per side. Remove from broiler, butter lightly, and top each half with 1 slice of ham.

4. Using a slotted spoon, remove eggs from the water in the same order that they were added, and set the spoon, with the egg inside, briefly on a clean kitchen towel to drain. Top each English muffin with a poached egg, and sprinkle with salt and pepper to taste. Serve immediately.

our favorite omelet fillings

Raw vegetables and meat must be precooked before they are combined with other ingredients in the following fillings.

- Finely grated cheese
- Smoked ham and tomatoes
- Goat cheese, roasted red peppers, and fresh thyme
- Cheddar cheese, tomatoes, and crumbled bacon
- Cooked chorizo sausage and minced green chiles
- Feta cheese, sautéed spinach, and cherry tomatoes

- Parmesan cheese and diced grilled vegetables
- Smoked salmon, shredded arugula, and cream cheese
- Brie, prosciutto, and steamed asparagus
- Monterey Jack cheese with prepared salsa
- Fresh mozzarella, tomatoes, and basil
- Gruyère cheese with sautéed red and yellow peppers

Boiled eggs can span a vast territory of textures (left). Some prefer the egg whites barely cooked, still translucent; others want them completely opaque, with the yolks starting to thicken. The perfect soft-boiled egg, of course, is one that's just the way you like it. Always have egg cups and spoons ready before you pluck your egg from the cooking pot of just-boiled water. With fork-tender whites and gloriously runny yolks, properly poached eggs (below) are a delight all by themselves, but why stop there? A couple of neatly trimmed poached eggs are perfect on buttered English muffin halves, with a slice of smoked or baked ham in the middle. For variation, top your muffin with wilted or creamed spinach, sautéed wild mushrooms, or a slice of juicy ripe tomato before sliding the warm eggs on top.

Spanish Onion and Potato Torta

7 tablespoons olive oil

1 medium Spanish onion (about 12 ounces), sliced into ¼-inch-thick half moons

3 medium Yukon gold or other floury potatoes (about 1 pound), sliced into ¼-inch-thick rounds

8 large eggs
 Salt and freshly ground pepper

1 twelve-inch-diameter round loaf rustic bread

1 clove garlic

1 small head frisée or other chicory lettuce

2 teaspoons sherry vinegar

This omelet, without a bread-loaf base, can also be cut into small pieces and served as a tapa or appetizer, either warm or at room temperature. **serves 6 to 8**

1. Heat oven to 325°. Heat 1 tablespoon of the oil in a 10-inch oven-safe skillet over medium-high heat. Add onion; sauté, stirring, until golden, 8 to 10 minutes. Transfer to a small bowl.

2. Return the skillet to heat, and add 1 tablespoon oil. Add potatoes, cover, and sauté until soft, stirring, 12 to 15 minutes. Transfer to the bowl with the onions, and combine.

3. Whisk together the eggs; add 1 teaspoon salt and a pinch of pepper. Transfer to the bowl with the onions and potatoes, and combine.

4. Return the skillet to the heat, and add 1 tablespoon oil. Add egg mixture, and cook until edges set and start to brown, about 1½ minutes. Cover, and bake in the oven until set, about 10 minutes. Remove cover, and broil until top is golden.

5. Meanwhile, slice the bread in half crosswise, and reserve the top half for another use. Remove some of the inside from bottom half, and discard crumb. Toast the bread under the broiler until golden. Remove, brush with 3 tablespoons oil, and rub with the garlic clove. Toss the frisée with the remaining tablespoon oil, vinegar, and a pinch of salt and pepper. Scatter the greens over the bread, and slide the torta over the greens. Cut in wedges, and serve.

A wedge of our version of a traditional thick round Spanish-style omelet makes a morning meal, with eggs, sautéed potatoes, and "toast" assembled in one hearty dish. We warmed a hollowed-out bread loaf, scattered seasoned frisée lettuce over it, and set the omelet on top.

Buttermilk Pancakes

2 cups all-purpose flour
2 teaspoons baking powder
1 teaspoon baking soda
1/2 teaspoon salt
3 tablespoons sugar
2 large eggs, lightly beaten
3 cups buttermilk
4 tablespoons plus 1/2 teaspoon
   unsalted butter, melted

Before heating up the griddle, see page 28 to learn how to make perfect pancakes. For blueberry pancakes, scatter a total of 1 cup fresh blueberries on top of the batter right after it has been poured on the griddle. Serve hot with fresh butter and pure maple syrup.   **makes nine 6-inch pancakes**

1. Heat an electric griddle to 375° or a heavy skillet until very hot. Whisk together flour, baking powder, baking soda, salt, and sugar in a medium bowl. Add eggs, buttermilk, and 4 tablespoons butter; whisk to combine. Batter should have small to medium lumps.

2. Heat oven to 175°. Test griddle by sprinkling a few drops of water on it. If water bounces and spatters off griddle, it is hot enough. Using a pastry brush, brush remaining 1/2 teaspoon butter onto the griddle. Wipe off excess with a folded paper towel.

3. Using a 4-ounce ladle, about 1/2 cup, pour pancake batter onto the hot griddle, in pools 2 inches away from each other. When pancakes have bubbles on top and are slightly dry around edges, about 2 1/2 minutes, flip over. Cook until golden on bottom, about 1 minute.

4. Repeat with remaining batter, keeping finished pancakes on a heat-proof plate in the oven.

what to put into your pancakes

For best results, add toppings to the pancakes once they have been poured onto the griddle. Nut and granola toppings will lose their crunch if they rest in the batter; other toppings will not be evenly distributed.

- Dried cherries and raisins plumped in fruit juice
- Chopped toasted pecans or walnuts
- Granola
- Sliced bananas

- Sliced peaches or pears and ground cardamom
- Apples and ground cinnamon
- Fresh raspberries or blackberries
- Poppy seeds and lemon zest

Our large Dutch Baby Pancake (right) is made like an upside-down cake, with a simple batter poured over honeyed apple pieces, then baked in a hot oven until puffed and golden. Serve in wedges, apples up, of course—with a dusting of confectioners' sugar. Other seasonal fruits can be used as well. Silver-Dollar Pear Pancakes (below) are individually griddle-baked, each sweet and savory coin containing a ring of maple-glazed pear. Arrange the small pancakes, overlapping, on a circular serving platter, surrounding a mound of sour cream sprinkled with cinnamon, with more maple syrup on the side.

Silver-Dollar Pear Pancakes

4 Bosc or Bartlett pears
3 tablespoons pure maple syrup, plus more for drizzling
¾ teaspoon ground cinnamon
½ teaspoon unsalted butter
1 recipe Buttermilk Pancakes batter (see recipe, page 25)
  Sour cream for garnish

The maple syrup keeps the pears from browning before cooking; it also adds flavor and creates a light glaze. This recipe can easily be halved.   **makes about two and one-half dozen 4-inch pancakes**

1. Core the pears with an apple corer. Starting at the bottom, slice pears crosswise into ⅛-inch-thick rings, and toss in a small bowl with the maple syrup and cinnamon.

2. Heat an electric griddle to 375° or a heavy skillet until very hot. Brush with butter; wipe off excess with a folded paper towel. Place a few pear slices on the griddle, 2½ inches apart. Let cook 1 minute. Ladle about ¼ cup of the batter into center of each pear ring. Using the bottom of a ladle, gently push batter over edges of pears. Let cook until pancakes have bubbles on top and are slightly dry around the edges, about 2½ minutes.

3. Using a spatula, turn pancakes over; cook until golden on bottom, about 1 minute. Repeat with remaining pears and batter. Serve with a dollop of sour cream and extra syrup.

Dutch Baby Pancake

1½ tablespoons unsalted butter
1 Granny Smith apple, peeled, cored, and cut into ½-inch wedges
⅓ cup honey
¼ teaspoon ground cardamom
3 large eggs
¾ cup milk
¾ cup all-purpose flour
¼ teaspoon salt
1 tablespoon confectioners' sugar

Baked in a large hot skillet, the thin eggy batter puffs up like a popover. To serve, slide the pancake from the skillet onto a round serving platter, and present it apple-side-up.   **serves 4**

1. Heat oven to 400°. Heat a well-seasoned 10-inch cast-iron skillet over high heat. Add butter. When melted, add apple wedges. Cook until softened and lightly golden, about 2 minutes. Stir in honey and cardamom, and remove skillet from heat.

2. In a separate bowl, whisk together remaining ingredients, except confectioners' sugar, until smooth. Pour over apple mixture. Bake until puffed and brown, about 20 minutes. Slide the pancake onto a serving platter. Serve immediately, cut into wedges, with confectioners' sugar sifted over the top.

"A teetering stack of silver-dollar pancakes, a pat of butter tucked between every layer—not just on top—and dripping with real maple syrup. That's the way to eat pancakes. Oh, and you must have bacon to dip in the syrup." —STEPHANA BOTTOM, SENIOR FOOD EDITOR

Perfect Pancakes

Making pancakes is among the simplest of culinary feats. To start, you need the right ingredients. Fortunately, the best flour for pancakes is also the most readily available — good old all-purpose. High-gluten flour makes tough, chewy pancakes, while pancakes made with cake flour get soggy when syrup is poured over them. For a change of taste, substitute cornmeal, buckwheat flour, or whole-wheat flour for half the all-purpose flour in our recipe for Buttermilk Pancakes (page 25).

1. When leavening with baking powder/soda, mixing the batter is critical. There are two stages: whisking together the dry ingredients, and whisking the wet ingredients into the dry. In the final step, don't whisk the batter to a smooth, uniform texture, or the gluten in the flour will develop and produce tough pancakes. Instead, mix the wet and dry ingredients together only partially, leaving lumps of unmoistened dry ingredients. The interaction of the liquid and the pockets of dry ingredients during cooking results in fluffy pancakes. Yeasted pancakes require no such care, but unless you want to wait for the batter to rise in the morning, mix it the night before, and let it rise in the refrigerator.

2. More butter does not mean better pancakes. A thin film covering the griddle prevents puddling and browns the pancakes evenly. After melting the butter on the griddle, wipe the surface with a paper towel. Too much melted butter on the griddle will result in "fried" pancakes—crispy on the outside and undercooked on the inside.

3. For fruit pancakes, place fruit on top of the batter right after it's poured onto the griddle. This allows the fruit to be evenly distributed in each pancake. Mixing the fruit in before the pancakes are on the griddle will thin the batter.

4. When is the time to flip? When the batter surface is covered with little bubbles, some of which have begun to break, the leavening agent has created enough carbon dioxide to lift and lighten the dough. The bursting bubbles, though, are letting that gas escape, so flip the pancake just at this moment, before too many have popped. Bubbles will appear first at the edges, which may begin to look dry before the rest of the surface is covered. Avoid the temptation to flip the pancake until some of the interior bubbles have burst.

The only way to make our best blueberry buttermilk pancakes even better: Stack them a mile high, slide soft pats of sweet butter in between each one, then drizzle warm maple syrup in a thick amber cascade over the top and down the sides, until the pool of syrup in your breakfast plate reaches the rim.

French doughnuts get their sheen from lemon-sugar glaze, curls of candied lemon zest, and poppy seeds. Made from the same egg-rich dough as cream puffs and éclairs, French doughnuts, or beignets, puff up when fried, gaining an airy texture without any special leaveners. Pipe the doughnuts into ring shapes using a pastry bag fitted with a star tip, giving each one fluted ridges to hold puddles of glaze.

French Doughnuts

2 quarts canola oil
2 cups all-purpose flour
2 cups milk
2 teaspoons coarse salt
2 teaspoons sugar
1 cup (2 sticks) unsalted
   butter, cut into small pieces
9 extra-large eggs
2½ teaspoons poppy seeds,
   plus more for sprinkling
   Lemon Glaze
   (recipe follows)
   Candied Lemon Zest
   (recipe follows)
   Vegetable-oil cooking spray

The dough can be piped or spooned into the frying oil to make round fritters, and dusted with confectioners' sugar or served with jam. **makes 30**

1. Cut thirty 4-inch squares out of parchment paper. Line two baking pans with paper towels. Heat oil in a low-sided six-quart saucepan over medium-high heat until a deep-frying thermometer registers 360°.

2. Meanwhile, sift the flour into a medium bowl. In a medium saucepan, combine the milk, salt, sugar, and butter. Bring to a full boil over medium-high heat. Remove from heat; add the sifted flour all at once, stirring constantly until flour has been incorporated. Return to heat; cook, stirring constantly, until the dough pulls away from sides, about 30 seconds. Remove pan from heat.

3. Transfer dough to the bowl of an electric mixer fitted with the paddle attachment. Beat on low speed until the bowl is warm to the touch, 4 to 5 minutes. Add eggs, one at a time, beating until each egg has been incorporated before adding the next. Stir in poppy seeds.

4. Coat a baking pan with the cooking spray, spread five squares of parchment on top, and generously spray parchment. Fit a large pastry bag with a #4 star tip; fill with dough. In one continuous stroke, pipe a 2½-inch double-layer circle onto each square.

5. Carefully lifting squares, gently slide five doughnuts into oil. Cook until golden brown, about 2 minutes. Using a slotted spoon, turn over; continue cooking until evenly browned, about 2 minutes more. Transfer to lined baking pans; let rest until cool enough to handle.

6. Repeat steps four and five with remaining parchment squares and dough.

7. Coat doughnuts with lemon glaze. Sprinkle with candied lemon zest and a pinch of poppy seeds. Transfer to a wire rack to set; serve.

Lemon Glaze   makes 1½ cups

2½ cups confectioners' sugar
¾ cup heavy cream
1 tablespoon plus 2 teaspoons freshly squeezed lemon juice (1 lemon)

Combine all the ingredients in a heat-proof bowl. Set over a pan of simmering water, and heat until just warm. Keep warm until ready to use.

Candied Lemon Zest   makes ½ cup

3 lemons
1¼ cups sugar
¼ cup light corn syrup

1. Using a zester, make 2-inch-long zest strips. Place zest in a small saucepan, cover with water, and bring to a boil. Cook 5 minutes, and drain in a fine sieve. Set zest aside.

2. Combine sugar, corn syrup, and 1½ cups water in a small saucepan; bring to a boil. Add zest; reduce heat to a simmer. Cook until translucent and tender, about 20 minutes. Remove from heat; let zest cool in liquid. Store, refrigerated, in an airtight container up to 1 week. Drain zest before using, discarding liquid.

Buttermilk Waffles

8 tablespoons (1 stick) butter, melted, plus more for greasing

2 cups all-purpose flour

¼ cup packed light-brown sugar

1 teaspoon baking soda

1½ teaspoons baking powder

½ teaspoon ground cinnamon

½ teaspoon salt

3 large eggs, separated, room temperature

2 cups buttermilk, room temperature

1 teaspoon pure vanilla extract

Serve warm with sweet butter and pure maple syrup. **serves 4 to 6**

1. Grease waffle iron with a small amount of melted butter, and heat. In a large bowl, sift together the flour, sugar, baking soda, baking powder, cinnamon, and salt.

2. In a separate bowl, whisk together egg yolks, buttermilk, 3 tablespoons melted butter, and vanilla. Pour into dry mixture, and combine.

3. In a medium bowl, beat the egg whites until stiff but not dry. Fold the whites into the batter (photo 1).

4. Ladle about ⅓ cup batter onto each section of the waffle grid; spread batter almost to the edges (photo 2). Close lid, and bake 3 to 5 minutes, until no steam emerges from waffle iron.

5. Transfer cooked waffles to a baking sheet; place in an oven set to low heat, about 200°, while using the remaining batter.

Cinnamon Sugar Waffles

¼ cup sugar

2 teaspoons ground cinnamon Buttermilk Waffle batter (recipe above)

The cinnamon sugar bakes into a sweet, crunchy topping when the lid of the waffle iron is closed. **serves 4 to 6**

1. In a small bowl, combine sugar and cinnamon; set aside.

2. Make batter, following steps one through three in the Buttermilk Waffles recipe above.

3. Ladle ⅓ cup batter onto each square of the waffle grid; spread almost to the edges. Sprinkle with 1 to 2 teaspoons cinnamon sugar (photo 3).

4. Close lid; bake 3 to 5 minutes, until no steam emerges from waffle iron. Transfer to a baking sheet; place in an oven set to low heat, about 200°, while using remaining batter. Serve warm.

Inspired by that childhood favorite, cinnamon toast, these sweet waffles fill the kitchen with the aroma of spice and vanilla. Keep waffles warm in a low oven while you prepare a whole stack. To serve, tuck upright in a towel-lined basket or, as we have done here, an antique painter's box. Serve butter, syrup, and more cinnamon-sugar on the side.

home for lunch

chapter two

There's no place like home for eating lunch the way you like it:

Slices of roasted pork loin, fresh from a warm oven, and fruit chutney fill a big crusty roll. Accompanied by wedges of baked acorn squash, the sandwich makes a hot and hearty lunch on an autumn afternoon. Fill up a tray with a platter of food, coarse-grained mustard, and good beer or sparkling cider, then settle down in the den to watch the occasional fall of a golden maple leaf.

sipping a big bowl of soothing tomato soup in front of the television, or nestling in your favorite armchair with a grilled-cheese sandwich and a good book.

The recipes in this chapter are for those people who like the idea of calling out "Soup's on!" or "Sandwiches are ready!" to the ones they love. These are dishes with ample pleasure for the hour you have before you all head to a matinee, or have to get to music lessons. You will find exceptional versions of lunchtime classics: a hot turkey sandwich with wild mushrooms and gravy, a best-ever tuna melt on a baguette, a gently spiced egg-salad picnic loaf, a towering bacon, lettuce, and tomato on brioche, and a golden grilled-cheese sandwich. And the essential soups of home cooking are here, too, in impeccable versions: creamy tomato, chicken noodle, matzo ball, French onion, and New England clam chowder.

Why don't we eat this way three meals a day? The truth is, some of us could.

An individual crock of French onion soup, its cheesy cap still bubbling from the broiler, is a glorious sight and makes a satisfying lunch all by itself. Although any ovenproof soup bowl can be used for serving, the extended rim of the traditional ceramic crock works best for forming a thick gratin, or crust, of toasted bread rounds and Gruyère.

French Onion Soup

4 tablespoons unsalted butter

2 pounds yellow onions, sliced
   ¼-inch into half circles

1 teaspoon sugar

1 tablespoon all-purpose flour

½ cup dry sherry

6 cups Homemade Beef Stock
   (recipe follows)

2 teaspoons chopped fresh thyme
   or ¾ teaspoon dried thyme
   Salt and freshly ground pepper

1 small French baguette, sliced
   crosswise into ½-inch pieces

8 ounces Gruyère cheese, grated on
   the large holes of a box grater
   to yield about 3 cups

Cooking the onions for a very long time over very low heat mellows their flavor. Don't stir them too often or they won't caramelize. This soup tastes best when made with Homemade Beef Stock.   **serves 6**

1. Melt butter in a large Dutch oven or heavy pot on medium-low heat. Add the onions. Spread them out in as thin a layer as possible. Sprinkle with sugar, and cook, stirring just as needed to keep the onions from sticking, until they are melting and soft, golden brown, and beginning to caramelize, about 1 hour.

2. Sprinkle the flour over the onions, and stir to coat. Add the sherry, stock, and thyme, and bring to a simmer. Cook, partially covered, for about 30 minutes, to allow the flavors to combine. Season with salt and pepper to taste.

3. Meanwhile, lightly toast the bread under a broiler; set aside. Ladle the hot soup into six ovenproof bowls. Arrange the bowls on a baking pan. Place 1 or 2 slices of toasted bread over each bowl of soup. Sprinkle ½ cup grated cheese over the bread in each bowl, and place under the broiler until the cheese is melted and crusty-brown around the edges. Watch carefully that the bread doesn't burn. Serve immediately.

Homemade Beef Stock

8 sprigs fresh flat-leaf parsley

6 sprigs fresh thyme or ¾
   teaspoon dried thyme

4 sprigs fresh rosemary or 2
   teaspoons dried rosemary

2 dried bay leaves

1 tablespoon whole black
   peppercorns

1 pound beef-stew meat, cubed

5 pounds veal bones, sawed into
   smaller pieces

1 large onion, peel on, quartered

2 large carrots, cut into thirds

2 stalks celery, cut into thirds

2 cups dry red wine

Homemade beef stock is far superior to store-bought, canned versions. Ask your butcher to saw the veal bones into smaller pieces.   **makes 6 quarts**

1. Heat the oven to 450°. Make a bouquet garni by wrapping the parsley, thyme, rosemary, bay leaves, and peppercorns in a piece of cheesecloth. Tie with kitchen twine, and set aside. Arrange the meat, veal bones, onion, carrots, and celery in an even layer in a heavy roasting pan. Roast, turning every 20 minutes, until the vegetables and the bones are deep brown, about 1½ hours. Transfer the meat, bones, and vegetables to a large stockpot, and set aside. Pour off the fat from the roasting pan, and discard. Place the pan over high heat on the stove. Add the wine, and use a wooden spoon to scrape up the brown bits; boil until the wine has reduced by half, about 5 minutes. Pour all of the liquid into the stockpot.

2. Add 6 quarts of cold water to the stockpot, or more if needed to cover bones. Do not add less water. Bring to a boil, then reduce to a very gentle simmer. Add the reserved bouquet garni. Liquid should just bubble up to surface. Skim the foam from the surface, and discard. Simmer over the lowest possible heat for 3 hours; a skin will form on the surface of the liquid; skim off with a slotted spoon, and discard. Repeat as needed. Add water if at any time the level drops below the bones.

3. Strain the stock through a fine sieve into a large bowl. Discard the solids. Transfer the bowl to an ice bath, and let cool to room temperature. Transfer to airtight containers. Refrigerate for at least 8 hours, or overnight. Stock may be refrigerated for 3 days or frozen for 4 months. If storing, leave fat layer intact to seal the stock. Before using, remove the fat that has collected on the surface.

Open-Face Turkey Sandwich With Mushroom Gravy

1 tablespoon unsalted butter

1 shallot, finely chopped

1 teaspoon fresh thyme leaves

1 pound mixed domestic and wild
mushrooms, such as shiitake,
oyster, or cremini, trimmed
and quartered
Salt and freshly ground pepper

1/2 cup Madeira wine

1 1/2 cups gravy (see Roast Turkey
Breast and Gravy recipe below)

4 thick slices white sandwich
bread, such as pain de
mie (Pullman)

3 pounds roast turkey breast
(1/2 Roast Turkey Breast and
Gravy recipe below)

1 small bunch watercress

This satisfying sandwich can be made with the recipe for Roast Turkey Breast and Gravy below or with your own turkey and gravy leftovers.   **makes 4 sandwiches**

1. Heat oven to 400°. Melt butter in a large skillet over medium heat. Add the shallot and thyme; cook until translucent, about 2 minutes. Add mushrooms; sauté until they release liquid and are soft, 3 to 5 minutes. Season with a pinch of salt and pepper. Add Madeira, raise heat to high, and sauté until liquid is cooked away, 3 to 5 minutes. Add gravy; cook until thick enough to coat the back of a spoon.

2. Meanwhile, slice turkey into about 1/4-inch-thick slices, and add to the gravy. Heat until turkey is hot, about 1 minute. Toast the bread under the broiler on both sides until golden but still soft.

3. Place toast on serving plates, spoon 1 or 2 tablespoons gravy over toast, and scatter watercress on top. Arrange turkey over toast, and spoon mushrooms and gravy over meat. Serve.

Roast Turkey Breast and Gravy

1 six-pound turkey breast

1 teaspoon salt, plus more to taste

1/4 teaspoon freshly ground pepper,
plus more to taste

3 large onions, sliced in half

3 carrots, sliced in half lengthwise

3 stalks celery

3 tablespoons all-purpose flour

1/4 cup Madeira wine, plus more
to taste

2 cups turkey stock or Chicken
Stock (recipe, page 56), or
canned

This makes enough turkey for eight open-face sandwiches. The meat will keep, double-wrapped in plastic, in the refrigerator for up to three days. Use it instead of chicken in Chicken Potpie (page 86) or add it to Chicken Noodle Soup (page 56).   **yields 1 turkey breast and 1 1/2 cups gravy**

1. Heat oven to 425°. Rinse turkey breast; pat dry. Rub breast with salt and pepper.

2. Scatter onions, carrots, and celery in a roasting pan; set turkey over vegetables. Roast until breast is cooked through, about 1 1/2 hours; a meat thermometer should register 170° when inserted into the thickest part of the breast.

3. Transfer half the breast to a cutting board. Tent with foil to warm; set aside.

4. Place roasting pan over two medium-hot burners on stove. Sprinkle cooked vegetables and drippings with flour, and cook, stirring constantly, until flour forms a golden-brown film over the bottom of the roasting pan and the vegetables are completely coated with film and turkey drippings, 2 to 3 minutes. Do not let pan get too hot or drippings will burn.

5. Pour Madeira slowly into pan, and cook, scraping up film from pan with a wooden spoon until a thin paste forms, about 1 minute. Slowly add stock, stirring, until paste thins to a thick liquid. Continue adding stock, stirring, until gravy is desired consistency. Season to taste with salt, pepper, and a splash more Madeira if desired. Strain gravy, pressing down on solids with rubber spatula to extract juices and flavor. Discard solids; transfer gravy to the top of double boiler to keep warm, or let cool and refrigerate. Serve warm.

Most open-face sandwiches require a knife and fork, and this sumptuous hot turkey sandwich is no exception. Sautéed mushrooms and a Madeira-wine gravy top slices of roasted meat, and a thick slice of toasted bread provides the foundation. Oven Frites make an unconventional side dish (recipe, page 100), though traditionalists might serve mashed potatoes instead (recipe, page 106).

Even meat lovers will enjoy
the textures and tang of this
vegetarian club. Layers of
mashed avocado, crunchy radish
slices, sprouts, and crumbled
goat cheese are perfect for a
springtime lunch break.

Avocado and Sprout Club Sandwich

12 slices white sandwich bread

2 ripe avocados

1 teaspoon salt

¼ teaspoon freshly ground pepper

1 bunch radishes, very thinly sliced

2 ounces alfalfa sprouts

8 ounces goat cheese, room temperature

Thinly sliced white sandwich bread should be soft and fresh. Use a homemade white or wheat bread, or a commercial home-style loaf. Select avocados that give slightly when pressed gently. If only firm avocados are available, buy them three days ahead so they can ripen.   **makes 4 double-decker sandwiches**

1. Place bread under the broiler, and toast until golden on both sides.

2. Prepare the avocado. Using an 8-inch chef's knife, cut to the pit, slicing the avocado all the way around the middle (photo 1). Twist top half off (photo 2). With a short, sharp but careful chopping motion, embed knife in pit; twist slightly, and remove pit from flesh (photo 3). Scoop flesh from skin with a large serving spoon, or peel both halves (photo 4).

3. Place avocado meat in a small bowl, and add salt and pepper. Using the back of a fork, mash the avocado into a chunky purée.

4. Spread the purée over 8 pieces of toast. Top with the radishes and sprouts. Crumble the goat cheese over sprouts.

5. Stack sandwiches together so that each sandwich has two layers of avocado, radish, sprouts, and goat cheese and three slices of toast. Cut in half, and serve immediately.

Everybody has her own way of constructing a BLT. We made this version with extra-generous layers—first buttery leaves of Bibb lettuce, then thin slices of vine-ripened tomatoes, and six whole strips of double-smoked thick-cut bacon. Then there's a layer of unexpected flavor: Our mayonnaise is mixed with a head of softly mashed, herb-roasted garlic and spread thickly onto the toasted pain de mie.

Scatter crisp, crumbled bacon bits and drizzle a spoonful of sherry into each bowl of steaming New England Clam Chowder, just before serving. Chowder lovers will appreciate the generous pieces of large quahog clams, whole pearl onions, and chunks of Yukon gold potatoes in our version of this national favorite.

The Best BLT

1 small head garlic

1 teaspoon olive oil

2 sprigs fresh thyme, rosemary, or oregano

½ cup mayonnaise

12 strips bacon

4 slices white sandwich bread, such as pain de mie (Pullman), sliced about ½ inch thick

1 small head Bibb or red-leaf lettuce

1 to 2 vine-ripened tomatoes, thinly sliced

Salt and freshly ground pepper

Look for dense, thickly cut white bread to support the layers of this sandwich, and use double-smoked, black pepper, or other flavorful bacon—it should be thickly cut, too.   **makes 2 sandwiches**

1. Heat oven to 375°. Rub entire head of garlic with olive oil. Place on aluminum foil, add herbs, and wrap tightly. Cook until cloves are soft, 25 to 35 minutes. Set aside to cool. Squeeze roasted garlic out of each clove onto a cutting board. Transfer soft garlic to a medium bowl; mash with a fork until smooth. Stir in mayonnaise, and set aside.

2. Working in batches, fry bacon in a heavy skillet over medium heat until crisp. Transfer bacon to paper towels to drain. Toast the bread under a broiler until lightly golden on both sides.

3. Spread one side of each bread slice with garlic mayonnaise. Arrange lettuce over two slices. Top with tomatoes and bacon. Season with salt and pepper. Top with remaining bread slices, and serve.

Cobb Club Sandwich

¼ cup olive oil

¼ cup balsamic vinegar

1 tablespoon Dijon mustard

2 whole boneless, skinless chicken breasts, trimmed of fat

Salt and freshly ground pepper

8 strips thick-cut bacon

12 slices brioche or challah

1 ripe avocado

Juice of ½ a lemon

⅓ cup mayonnaise

1 head green-leaf lettuce

1 tomato, thinly sliced

½ pound blue cheese, crumbled

We've sliced rather than chopped the ingredients of a Cobb salad in this sandwich version of one of America's great salads.   **makes 4 double-decker sandwiches**

1. Combine oil, vinegar, and mustard in a small bowl. Season chicken with salt and pepper, and place in the bowl, stirring to coat. Marinate, covered, for at least a half an hour.

2. Cook chicken on a hot grill for 7 minutes on each side, or until cooked through. Let cool slightly; slice thinly at an angle.

3. In a large heavy skillet over medium heat, cook bacon until crisp, and drain on paper towels. Toast the bread under a broiler until lightly golden on both sides. Quarter and thinly slice the avocado, and drizzle with the lemon juice to prevent discoloration.

4. Assemble the sandwich in this order: bread, mayonnaise, lettuce, tomato, avocado, bread, mayonnaise, chicken, bacon, cheese, mayonnaise, bread. Serve immediately.

The intense flavors of tangy blue cheese, marinated grilled chicken, and smoky bacon are complemented by layered slices of creamy avocado, crisp lettuce, juicy tomatoes, and airy brioche. You'll need both hands to hold on to this double-decker Cobb Club Sandwich, inspired by the salad made famous at the Brown Derby Restaurant in Hollywood.

Summer Corn Chowder

4 ounces bacon, cut into ¼-inch
dice

1 small onion, peeled and cut into
¼-inch dice (1 cup)

2 ribs celery, strings removed, cut
into ½-inch dice (¾ cup)

8 sprigs fresh thyme
Salt and freshly ground pepper

3 cups Chicken Stock (recipe,
page 56), or canned

3 ears yellow corn, kernels removed (about 2½ cups)

5 ounces small fingerling potatoes,
cut into ½-inch-thick slices

1 poblano chile, seeded and cut into
½-inch dice

1½ cups half-and-half

Fresh corn, cut off the cob, provides natural sweetness, while fresh thyme and poblano chile lend layers of subtle flavor to this simple, quick-cooking chowder. **serves 4**

1. Place the bacon in a small stockpot over medium-high heat. Cook the bacon, stirring occasionally, until it is deep golden brown and all the fat has been rendered, about 4 minutes. Remove the bacon with a slotted spoon, then transfer to paper towels to drain, and set aside. Discard all but 2 tablespoons of the bacon fat.

2. Add the diced onion, celery, thyme, and salt and pepper to taste to stockpot; cook over medium-low heat until translucent, about 8 minutes. Add stock; bring to a boil. Reduce heat to medium, and simmer 15 minutes.

3. Add the corn, potato slices, and poblano chile; cook until the potatoes are tender, 8 to 10 minutes. Remove from heat. Using a slotted spoon, remove and discard thyme. Add the half-and-half, and simmer until soup is hot. Taste and adjust seasoning with salt and pepper. Ladle the soup into soup bowls, and garnish with the bacon. Serve immediately.

New England Clam Chowder

6 strips bacon, cut into 1-inch
pieces

2 ribs celery, strings removed, cut
into ¼-inch dice

1 cup small pearl onions, peeled

3 tablespoons all-purpose flour

2 cups unsalted clam juice

4 small Yukon gold potatoes (about
1 pound), peeled and cut into ½-
inch dice

2 dried bay leaves

¼ teaspoon freshly ground pepper

5 large sprigs fresh thyme

8 pounds quahog clams, shucked,
liquid reserved, and chopped into
½-inch pieces (2 pounds shucked)

2 ears fresh yellow corn

2½ cups milk

2 tablespoons unsalted butter

1 teaspoon salt

1 tablespoon dry sherry (optional)

Sautéing the vegetables in the bacon drippings gives this thick chowder extra flavor. **serves 6 to 8**

1. In a stockpot, cook the bacon until crisp. Drain the bacon on a paper towel, and set aside; discard all but 2 tablespoons of the bacon fat. Add the celery and onions; sauté, stirring occasionally with a wooden spoon, until translucent, about 7 minutes.

2. Sprinkle flour over onion mixture; cook, stirring with a wooden spoon, 2 to 3 minutes. Add clam juice, ½ cup water, potatoes, bay leaves, and ⅛ teaspoon of the pepper; cover; bring to a boil. Pick thyme leaves from stems; add both leaves and stems to pot. Reduce heat to medium low; simmer until potatoes are almost fork tender, about 12 minutes.

3. Add clams and reserved liquid, cover, and cook 4 minutes over medium heat. Add corn, cover, and cook 4 to 6 minutes. Add milk and butter; cook until butter melts, about 5 minutes. Remove bay leaves and thyme stems; add remaining ⅛ teaspoon pepper and salt.

4. Drizzle with sherry and garnish with bacon pieces. Serve immediately.

You will need a crusty country roll or a square of homemade focaccia to hold the ingredients and to absorb all the flavorful juices in this smoky warm sandwich. Black-olive spread, sautéed artichokes, and tomatoes are infused with olive oil, garlic, and parsley, piled in the roll, then crowned with Taleggio cheese.

Mediterranean Melt

3 lemons

8 baby artichokes

1/2 cup oil-cured black olives, pitted and coarsely chopped

1/4 cup olive oil

1 small clove garlic, minced
Salt and freshly ground pepper

1 cup loosely packed fresh flat-leaf parsley leaves, roughly chopped

4 ripe plum tomatoes, sliced 3/4 inch thick

4 rustic-style rolls or 1 recipe Homemade Focaccia (recipe below), cut in quarters

1/2 pound Taleggio or fontina cheese, sliced 1/4 inch thick

When using focaccia to make this melt, try grilling the entire sandwich in a hot skillet over medium-high heat until both sides are golden brown.   **makes 4 sandwiches**

1. Slice 2 lemons in half, and squeeze juice into a bowl of cold water. Add lemon halves to bowl.

2. Trim tips and outer leaves from artichokes; slice thinly, lengthwise; submerge in the lemon water. Combine olives with 1 tablespoon oil in a small bowl, and set aside.

3. Heat 1 1/2 tablespoons oil in a skillet over medium heat; add the garlic. Sauté until fragrant, about 30 seconds. Pat artichokes dry; add to skillet. Sauté until golden, about 5 minutes. Squeeze juice of remaining lemon over artichokes; season with a pinch of salt and pepper, and add 1/2 cup chopped parsley; toss. Transfer to a small bowl; cover with foil.

4. Return skillet to heat; add remaining 1 1/2 tablespoons oil. Arrange tomatoes in skillet. Season with salt and pepper; sprinkle with remaining 1/2 cup parsley. Cook until golden around edges, about 5 minutes. Turn over, and sauté 1 to 2 minutes more.

5. Slice the rolls or focaccia open; scoop out bottom, creating a cavity for the filling; spread with olive mixture. Mound the artichoke mixture over olives. Arrange tomatoes over the artichokes. Arrange the cheese over the tomatoes. Place sandwich halves and the tops, crumb side up, on baking sheet; broil until cheese melts and bread is golden, about 2 minutes. Close sandwiches. Serve.

Home-Baked Focaccia

Pinch of sugar

2 teaspoons active dry yeast

2 tablespoons olive oil, plus more for bowl, baking sheet, and drizzling

6 cups all-purpose flour, or half all-purpose and half bread flour

1 tablespoon coarse salt, plus more for sprinkling
Fresh rosemary (optional)

This large sheet of homemade focaccia has many delicious uses. It is a superb alternative to rustic-style rolls in a Mediterranean Melt (recipe above) and other sandwiches, and it is a fine complement to soups and main-course dishes, too.   **makes one 12-by-18-inch loaf**

1. In a large bowl, stir sugar into 1/4 cup warm water, and sprinkle in the yeast. Stir well; let stand until creamy, about 10 minutes.

2. Add 2 1/2 cups warm water and the olive oil, and mix well. Add the flour, 1 cup at a time, mixing well. Add salt, and knead dough until smooth and elastic, 4 to 5 minutes by electric mixer or 8 to 10 minutes by hand.

3. Form dough into a ball, and place in a lightly oiled bowl. Cover with plastic wrap, and let rise at room temperature until doubled in bulk, 1 to 1 1/2 hours.

4. Spread dough evenly onto an oiled baking sheet. Cover with a damp towel, and let rise 30 minutes.

5. Dimple surface of dough with your fingertips, leaving deep indentations. Cover with towel again, and let rise until doubled, 1 1/2 to 2 hours.

6. Heat oven to 425°. Drizzle oil on top of dough, allowing dimples to fill. Using a pastry brush, gently spread oil over surface without deflating dough. Brush lightly with water, then sprinkle with the salt and rosemary, if desired.

7. Bake for 25 to 30 minutes, or until golden brown. Remove from oven, and slide onto a wire rack. Serve as soon as possible.

Matzo balls are easy-to-make soup dumplings, traditionally eaten during Passover, but floating in a rich chicken broth, they make a satisfying meal any time of year. The stock, matzo balls, and carrots and parsnip can be cooked ahead of time and reheated for lunch.

Matzo Ball Soup

3 large eggs

3 tablespoons rendered chicken fat (available at butcher shops or in the meat departments of large supermarkets) or vegetable oil

1½ teaspoons coarse salt

¾ cup plus 2 tablespoons matzo meal

½ recipe Chicken Stock (recipe, page 56) (10 cups), or canned

3 medium carrots, peeled and sliced into ½-inch-thick rounds

2 medium parsnips, peeled and sliced into ½-inch-thick rounds
Fresh dill, for garnish

Cooking the matzo balls in the chicken stock may make the soup a bit cloudy, but the matzo balls will soak up flavor from the rich broth. If you desire a clearer soup, simply strain out the cooked matzo balls and vegetables, and heat them in the remaining chicken stock.   serves 4 to 6

1. In a medium bowl, whisk together the eggs and the chicken fat until combined. Whisk in ½ cup water and the salt. Add the matzo meal and whisk until combined. Cover and refrigerate batter until firm, 2 to 4 hours.

2. Line a baking pan with parchment. Bring the chicken stock to a boil in a large wide saucepan, and reduce heat to a simmer.

3. Slightly dampen your fingertips and form 2 heaping tablespoons of batter into a 1½-inch ball, being careful not to compress the mixture too much. Place the ball on the prepared pan. Repeat process with the remaining batter.

4. Using a large spoon, slide the matzo balls into the simmering stock. Once all the balls have been added, cover and cook for 10 minutes. Add the carrots and parsnips, cover, and continue cooking for 20 to 25 minutes, until the vegetables are tender and the matzo balls are cooked through. To test if the matzo balls are done, remove a ball from the water, and slice in half. The color should be light throughout. If the center is darker, cook 5 to 10 minutes more.

5. To serve, fill the soup bowls evenly with soup and vegetables, allotting each person 1 or 2 matzo balls, depending on his or her appetite. Garnish with the fresh dill, and serve immediately.

"I still wonder how such delicate chicken broth and perfect matzo balls came from Aunt Buddy's tiny kitchen. It was so chaotic! All those big pots steaming on the stove. Now I go to the 2nd Avenue Deli for Chicken in the Pot, a jar full of the good things I remember. Except the steam. I miss the steam." —SUSAN SPUNGEN, FOOD EDITOR

Creamy Tomato Soup

2 tablespoons unsalted butter
1 medium onion, finely chopped
3 cloves garlic, minced
3 26½-ounce boxes vacuum-packed
   crushed tomatoes or 10 cups
   canned crushed tomatoes
5¼ cups Chicken Stock
   (recipe, page 56) or canned
3 sprigs fresh oregano, plus more
   for garnish
½ cup half-and-half
   Salt and freshly ground pepper

This tomato soup is also delicious without the half-and-half—or with twice as much!   **serves 6 to 8**

1. Melt the butter in a medium saucepan over medium-low heat. Add the onion and garlic, and cook, stirring, until translucent, about 6 minutes.

2. Add the tomatoes, stock, and oregano, and bring to a boil. Reduce heat, and simmer gently until thickened, about 45 minutes. Remove oregano sprigs.

3. Slowly add half-and-half, stirring constantly. Season with salt and pepper. Garnish with oregano, if desired. Serve hot.

Grilled Cheese Sandwich

4 slices white sandwich bread,
   such as pain de mie (Pullman),
   about ½-inch thick
   Monterey Jack cheese, cut in
   ⅛-inch-thick slices
   (about 2 ounces)
   Cheddar cheese, cut in
   ⅛-inch-thick slices
   (about 2 ounces)
   Unsalted butter,
   room temperature

If you use thinner, presliced sandwich bread, you will need to reduce the amount of cheese and butter in the sandwich. Instead, use 1½ ounces of cheese per sandwich (using a single layer of cheese) and coat the outer sides of the bread with a little less butter.   **makes 2 sandwiches**

1. Heat a large cast-iron or heavy metal skillet over medium-low heat. Place two slices of bread on a work surface, and cover each with a layer of Monterey Jack and a layer of cheddar cheese; top with the remaining slices of bread. Generously butter both outer sides of the sandwiches, spreading butter all the way to the edges of the bread.

2. Place the sandwiches in the skillet, and press down only lightly with the back of a spatula. Cook until golden brown on each side, 3 to 4 minutes per side, and the cheese has completely melted. Cut in half lengthwise, and serve immediately.

what could be better than classic grilled cheese?

Martha's favorite way to make one for herself is to coat the inside of bread with Dijon mustard and insert sweet gherkins thinly sliced lengthwise between the layers of Monterey Jack and cheddar cheese. Other staff members offer the following variations:

- Cheddar cheese, thick slices of ripe tomato, and crisp bacon
- Gruyère cheese, thinly sliced ham, and whole-grain mustard
- Fresh mozzarella, tomatoes, and basil leaves
- Fontina cheese, black-olive paste, and prosciutto
- Manchego and Monterey Jack cheeses and pickled jalapeño peppers

- Taleggio cheese with grilled red peppers and zucchini
- Brie, smoked turkey breast, and sliced pears
- Blue cheese with sliced apples
- Blue cheese, crisp bacon, and tomatoes
- Swiss cheese, thinly sliced cooked potatoes, and caramelized onions

A basic Grilled-Cheese Sandwich is always what you want—thick-sliced white bread, layers of cheddar and Monterey Jack cheese, pan-toasted to buttery crispness on the outside and melting richness within. You can make all kinds of additions to the sandwich itself (see sidebar, opposite), but a frosty chocolate milk shake on the side will capture its essence. A mug of Creamy Tomato Soup (below) is a hand- and heart-warming cold-weather favorite. Our version is thick with crushed tomatoes and laced with garlic and oregano— a tangy complement to wedges of grilled-cheese sandwich.

Tastes, textures, and colors mingle in a deep bowl of golden squash soup. Purée just half the soup after the brief cooking so there are plenty of soft chunks of leek, parsnip, and butternut squash remaining, then add crispy whole-wheat Parmesan croutons. Fresh ginger and garlic add pungent accents to the naturally sweet vegetable flavors.

Wedges of Egg Salad Sandwich, cut from country bread, make a quick and convenient lunch for a crowd, at a backyard picnic, or at the kitchen table. Spread a generous amount of filling between the layers of a round of whole-wheat peasant bread. Then serve it right on the cutting board with a serrated knife nearby so guests can help themselves.

Roasted Pork Loin With Warm Fruit Chutney

1   two-pound pork loin
1   tablespoon olive oil
1½ teaspoons salt
¼   teaspoon freshly ground pepper
1   tablespoon fresh thyme leaves
¾   cup fruit chutney
4   rustic-style rolls
2   tablespoons grainy mustard

Fruit chutney is available in most supermarkets. Look for the chunkiest version you can find.   **makes 4 sandwiches**

1. Heat oven to 400°. Rub meat with oil; sprinkle with the salt, pepper, and thyme. Roast in small pan until a meat thermometer inserted into the thickest part of the meat registers 160°, about 1¼ hours. Tent with foil to keep warm; let stand.

2. Place the chutney in a small saucepan over medium heat until very warm. Set aside.

3. Slice the rolls open, and spread with the mustard. Slice the meat into ¼-inch-thick slices, and arrange over the bottom halves of the rolls. Top with the warm chutney. Cover with the tops of the rolls, and place on a baking sheet. Transfer to the oven, and heat until rolls are toasty and filling is hot, about 5 minutes. Serve immediately.

Ginger Squash Soup With Parmesan Croutons

2¾ pounds orange-flesh winter
    squash, such as butternut
2   tablespoons olive oil
1   medium leek, trimmed; white and
    green parts cut into ¼-inch
    pieces to yield 1 cup
3   cloves garlic, peeled and minced
1   teaspoon finely grated fresh
    ginger, or more to taste
4   ounces parsnips (1 medium),
    peeled and cut into ¼-inch pieces
1   teaspoon salt, plus more to taste
¼   teaspoon freshly ground pepper
    plus more to taste
4   cups Chicken Stock (recipe,
    page 56), or canned
2   three-quarter-inch slices whole-
    wheat bread, crusts removed
3   tablespoons freshly grated
    Parmesan cheese

This full-flavored soup is remarkably low in fat, and can be completed in less than an hour. Use an immersion blender, if you have one, to partially purée the soup.   **serves 6**

1. Cut the squash in half lengthwise. Remove the seeds and fiber, and peel. Cut into ½-inch pieces, and set aside.

2. Heat the olive oil in a large stockpot over medium-low heat. Cook the leek and garlic until softened, 3 to 5 minutes. Add the ginger, squash, and parsnips. Stir, and cook over medium heat 3 to 5 minutes. Add the salt, pepper, and stock. Cover, and bring to a boil. Reduce to a simmer, and cook until the squash and parsnips are tender, 12 to 15 minutes. Transfer half the mixture to a food processor, and purée. Return to the stockpot until warm throughout. Adjust the seasoning to taste with salt and pepper.

3. Meanwhile, cut the bread into ½-inch cubes. Toast under the broiler until golden brown. Sprinkle with the Parmesan, and return to the broiler, until the cheese begins to melt. Serve the soup in individual bowls with the toasted-cheese croutons on top.

Alexis's Egg Salad Sandwich

6 hard-boiled eggs, peeled, roughly chopped

¼ cup mayonnaise, plus more for spreading

½ teaspoon dry mustard powder, or ¾ teaspoon Dijon mustard

3 tablespoons diced celery
Salt and freshly ground pepper

¼ teaspoon mild Madras curry powder (optional)

1 eight-inch round bread loaf, cut in half crosswise
Dijon mustard, for spreading (optional)

1 small head radicchio

1 small bunch arugula

Martha loves her daughter's egg salad—mustard powder gives it a balance of flavor, while Dijon adds a zestier note. Use a good quality whole-wheat bread. **serves 6 to 8**

1. In a medium bowl, combine the eggs, mayonnaise, mustard powder, celery, salt, and pepper to taste, and the curry powder, if using. Gently mix until combined.

2. Spread the inside of the bread halves with a layer of mayonnaise and mustard, if using. Line the bottom half with radicchio and arugula leaves, and top with the egg salad. Cover with the top half, and cut the sandwich into wedges. Serve immediately.

Two-Bite Tuna Melt

1 demi baguette, cut in half lengthwise
Mayonnaise, for spreading (optional)

2 recipes Tuna Salad (recipe follows)
Monterey Jack or white cheddar cheese, thinly sliced (about 6 ounces)

4 fresh basil leaves, thinly sliced (optional)

Spread the toast with a layer of mustard for a spicier sandwich, or add a slice of tomato for juicy sweetness. This tuna melt can also be made with rye or white sandwich bread. **serves 4**

1. Set a rack in the top third of the oven, and heat the broiler.

2. On a cookie sheet, toast the bread halves under the broiler until lightly golden on both sides. Transfer to a work surface.

3. If using, spread the bread with mayonnaise. Top each half with tuna salad and a single layer of cheese.

4. Return the open-faced sandwiches to the cookie sheet, and broil, watching carefully, until the cheese is completely melted, about 1½ minutes. Cut each piece of bread in half for 4 sandwiches, or into one-to-two-inch slices for easy nibbling. Garnish with fresh basil, if using, and serve.

1 six-ounce can water-packed tuna, drained

2 tablespoons mayonnaise

1 teaspoon Dijon mustard

2 tablespoons finely minced celery

1 teaspoon freshly squeezed lemon juice

1 teaspoon grated lemon zest
Salt and freshly ground pepper

Tuna Salad   **makes 2 servings (about ¾ cup)**

In a medium bowl, combine the tuna, mayonnaise, mustard, celery, lemon juice, zest, and salt and pepper to taste. Using a fork, mix well until thoroughly combined. Store in an airtight container in the refrigerator up to 1 day.

Chicken Noodle Soup

3 quarts Chicken Stock
(recipe follows), or canned

3 carrots, cut into ⅛-inch-thick
rounds
Salt and freshly ground pepper

8 ounces medium egg noodles
Cooked chicken meat,
shredded (see Chicken Stock,
recipe follows)

¼ cup chopped fresh dill or
1 tablespoon dried dill

¼ cup chopped fresh flat-leaf
parsley

1 teaspoon whole black
peppercorns

6 sprigs fresh dill or 2 teaspoons
dried dill

6 sprigs fresh flat-leaf parsley

2 dried bay leaves

2 leeks, washed, white and pale-
green parts only, cut into thirds

2 carrots, scrubbed, cut into thirds

2 stalks celery, cut into thirds

1 4-pound chicken, cut into 6
pieces

1½ pounds chicken wings

1½ pounds chicken backs

12 cups low-sodium canned chicken
stock (two 48-ounce cans)

In addition to broad egg noodles, you can make this heavenly soup with angel-hair pasta broken into short lengths or other shapes, such as alphabet pasta or pastina, or add cooked grains like rice.   **makes 3¼ quarts**

1. Place stock in a stockpot 1over medium-high heat, and bring just to a simmer. Add carrots and simmer until tender, about 6 minutes.

2. Meanwhile, bring a large saucepan of salted water to a boil. Cook the noodles until just tender, about 6 minutes. Drain the noodles and add them to the pot of stock, along with the shredded chicken meat. Season with salt and pepper. Heat until very hot. When ready to serve, stir in dill and parsley.

Chicken Stock

This recipe makes more than you'll need for Chicken Noodle Soup or Matzo Ball Soup. The stock can be frozen up to four months. The gelatin from the chicken bones is released during the long cooking time yielding a rich, flavorful stock.   **makes 5 quarts**

1. Place the peppercorns, dill, parsley, bay leaves, leeks, carrots, celery, chicken, wings, and backs into a large stockpot. Add the stock and 6 cups of cold water. Bring to a boil. Reduce to a very gentle simmer, and cook for 45 minutes. Liquid should just bubble up to the surface. A skin will form on the surface of the liquid; skim off with a slotted spoon, and discard. Repeat as needed. After 45 minutes, remove the chicken from the pot, and set aside until it is cool enough to handle.

2. Remove the meat from the bones, set the meat aside, and return the bones to the pot. Shred the chicken, and set aside in the refrigerator until ready to use. (Chicken meat is used to make Chicken Noodle Soup, recipe above, or can be added to Matzo Ball Soup, recipe page 49.) Continue to simmer the stock, on the lowest heat possible, for 3 hours, skimming as needed. The chicken bones will begin to disintegrate. Strain the stock through a fine sieve into a very large bowl. Discard the solids. Place the bowl in an ice bath, and let cool to room temperature. Transfer to airtight containers. Stock may be refrigerated for 3 days or frozen for 4 months. Refrigerate for at least 8 hours, or overnight. If storing, leave fat layer intact to the seal the stock. Before using, remove the layer of fat that has collected on the surface.

A brimming tureen of chicken-
noodle soup is a feast for all the
senses—and a magical reviver
of flagging spirits. All the soup
components can be prepared
separately, then heated together
when you are ready to eat.
The final garnish of fresh dill
and parsley should be added
when serving, to release their
wonderful, stimulating aroma.

what to have for dinner

chapter three

What do Americans have for dinner?

A supper for all seasons: A glass of red wine and a big bowl of spaghetti flecked with fresh basil and coated with tomato sauce that is garlicky but light. When making the sauce, you can use sweet cherry and pear tomatoes or vine-ripened tomatoes in the summer, or good-quality canned ones in winter. It takes just minutes; there's no need to start cooking the sauce until you drop the spaghetti into the pot.

Almost anything we want. Whether we crave Moroccan lamb stew, a sushi roll, or a bowl of Vietnamese beef soup, we can find it. We inhabit a culinary melting pot of markets, restaurants, chefs, and neighbors who bring us every taste from every corner of the earth.

But if you ask someone in Tangiers or Tokyo what Americans have for dinner—or any American under the age of 10 what he wants for dinner—he will likely say a hamburger, fried chicken, or pizza. And that answer is right, too. Even with a world of choices, we cherish with fierce loyalty our American supper favorites—a category that includes spaghetti, mac-

aroni, and meat loaf. These are the dishes we eat week in and week out throughout our lives; we make them at home, we order them at restaurants, and, when we need speed and reassurance, they're what we take out.

There are many reasons why these simple-to-make dishes have become our nation's classics, symbols of our cooking the world around. But there's no mystery why they comfort us: They always taste good. And with the wonderful versions that we give you here, they'll never taste better.

Macaroni and Cheese

8 tablespoons (1 stick) unsalted butter, plus more for dish

6 slices good-quality white bread, crusts removed, torn into ¼-to-½-inch pieces

5½ cups milk

½ cup all-purpose flour

2 teaspoons salt

¼ teaspoon freshly grated nutmeg

¼ teaspoon freshly ground black pepper

¼ teaspoon cayenne pepper

4½ cups (about 18 ounces) grated sharp white cheddar cheese

2 cups (about 8 ounces) grated Gruyère or 1¼ cups (about 5 ounces) grated Pecorino Romano cheese

1 pound elbow macaroni

You can easily divide this recipe in half: Use a one-and-a-half-quart casserole dish.   **serves 12**

1. Heat the oven to 375°. Butter a 3-quart casserole dish, and set aside. Place the bread pieces in a medium bowl. In a small saucepan over medium heat, melt 2 tablespoons butter. Pour the butter into the bowl with the bread, and toss. Set the bread crumbs aside. In a medium saucepan set over medium heat, heat the milk. Melt remaining 6 tablespoons butter in a high-sided skillet over medium heat. When the butter bubbles, add the flour. Cook, stirring, 1 minute.

2. Slowly pour in the hot milk while whisking. Continue cooking, whisking constantly, until the mixture bubbles and becomes thick.

3. Remove the pan from the heat. Stir in the salt, nutmeg, black pepper, cayenne pepper, 3 cups cheddar cheese, and 1½ cups Gruyère or 1 cup Pecorino Romano. Set cheese sauce aside.

4. Fill a large saucepan with water. Bring to a boil. Add macaroni; cook 2 to 3 minutes less than manufacturer's directions, until outside of pasta is cooked and inside is underdone. (Different brands of macaroni cook at different rates; be sure to read the instructions.) Transfer the macaroni to a colander, rinse under cold running water, and drain well. Stir macaroni into the reserved cheese sauce.

5. Pour the mixture into the prepared casserole dish. Sprinkle remaining 1½ cups cheddar and ½ cup Gruyère or ¼ cup Pecorino Romano; scatter bread crumbs over the top. Bake until browned on top, about 30 minutes. Transfer the dish to a wire rack to cool 5 minutes, and serve.

 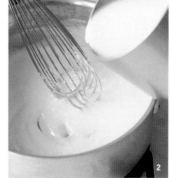  

A thick cheddar and Gruyère white sauce makes this Macaroni and Cheese more interesting than most. Fresh buttered bread crumbs add a crown of crunch and color. Serve hot, accompanied by a green salad of crisp romaine and tangy arugula.

Some people like to use a spoon, too, but a twirl of the fork will do. Coated with fresh tomato sauce, this spaghetti is tangled with slivers of tomato, garlic, and basil. Shreds of grated Parmigiano-Reggiano cheese cling to the warm strands. Polite slurping may be acceptable.

Spaghetti With Tomato Sauce

2 tablespoons plus ¼ teaspoon
coarse salt

1½ pounds baby pear (or cherry)
tomatoes or vine-ripened tomatoes, or 1 twenty-eight-ounce
can Italian plum tomatoes

8 ounces thin best-quality spaghetti

¼ cup extra-virgin olive oil

4 cloves garlic, cut into ⅛-inch-
thick pieces

¼ teaspoon crushed red-pepper
flakes

¼ cup fresh basil or parsley leaves,
loosely packed and torn
Parmigiano-Reggiano cheese,
grated (optional)

This recipe's quickness depends on getting all the sauce ingredients and cooking equipment ready before you start cooking. Then, when the water's boiling, start the pasta, and sauté the sauce at the same time. See illustrated instructions, page 64.   **serves 2 to 4**

1. In a tall stockpot, bring 3 quarts of water and 2 tablespoons salt to a boil.

2. In a separate pot, prepare the tomatoes following steps 1, 2, or 3 on page 64. Set aside.

3. Drop spaghetti into boiling salted water; stir. Cook until al dente, about 11 minutes.

4. Place a 12-inch sauté pan over medium heat, and add the oil. Add the garlic to the pan. Cook, stirring occasionally, until garlic is lightly golden, about 30 seconds. Add the red-pepper flakes and remaining ¼ teaspoon salt. Cook until the garlic is medium golden, about 1 minute.

5. Increase heat to high. Tilting pan at an angle, add the reserved tomatoes. Cook, swirling pan occasionally, until the tomatoes begin to break down, pear tomatoes begin to burst, or canned tomatoes begin to thicken, 5 to 6 minutes. If using pear tomatoes, mash a few with a spoon. If pear tomatoes start to get too dry, add a little water from the stockpot.

6. Drain pasta in a colander, reserving 1 cup liquid in case sauce gets too dry when pasta is added. Add pasta to sauce in sauté pan. Cook until the sauce begins to cling to pasta, 3 to 4 minutes. Stir in the basil; cook 30 seconds more. Divide among bowls, and sprinkle with cheese, if desired. Serve.

what to toss with your spaghetti

A steaming bowl of spaghetti is a testament to simply delicious food. But not everyone is satisfied with just tomato sauce. If you yearn for that extra something in your pasta, try these favorite "add-ins" with your next spaghetti dinner. Always reserve a little pasta-cooking water to toss in and moisten the ingredients.

- Sweet butter, coarse salt, and freshly ground pepper
- Crumbled Italian sausage
- Parmesan cheese, roasted garlic, and freshly ground pepper
- Pitted black or green olives
- Chopped fresh herbs
- Sautéed mushrooms and chopped fresh tarragon
- Crisp pancetta, green peas, and a drizzle of heavy cream

- Marinated artichoke hearts
- Crumbled goat cheese
- Grilled eggplant and zucchini chunks
- Steamed asparagus, toasted pine nuts, and lemon zest
- Chopped anchovies
- Cubes of fresh mozzarella with fresh tomatoes
- Extra-virgin olive oil

Spaghetti 101

Spaghetti with tomato sauce seems like the simplest meal, and it is. But it's as easy to do it wrong as it is to do it right. The simpler the dish, the more important it is that you use the highest-quality ingredients. Technique and timing are also critical, but not at all difficult. The quick method described here is not meant to replace the slow-simmered sauce favored by Italian grandmothers. If you're lucky enough to be given the recipe for Grandma's sauce, by all means take it. Except for the short time of year when fresh tomatoes are at their peak, imported Italian plum tomatoes are your best choice. For the most delicious flavor, look in supermarkets and specialty-food stores for San Marzano tomatoes, which are a type of Italian tomato, not a brand. Yellow and red baby pear tomatoes make a delicious variation. If your tomatoes are very sweet, try using flat-leaf parsley instead of basil to balance the flavors. Whichever tomatoes you choose, pay attention to the tips given here for a deeply satisfying meal.

1. Fresh tomatoes should be peeled and seeded for best results. Bring a large pot of water (3 quarts) to a rolling boil. Add 2 tablespoons salt; use this water to loosen the skins. Cut a small "X" in the bottom of each tomato, and drop one or two at a time into boiling water, just until the skin begins to curl back at the "X." Lift out of water with skimmer, and drop into an ice-water bath to stop the cooking. If skins do not slip right off, return to boiling water for a few seconds more. Use a sharp knife to cut the outside fleshy part of the tomatoes in large pieces, and cut them into strips. Place seedy pulp in a sieve; push it through with a rubber spatula.

2. Cook yellow and red baby pear tomatoes and cherry tomatoes in the same way and for the same amount of time as for fresh tomatoes. When the tomatoes begin to burst, use the back of a spoon to crush some of them even more, which will help to thicken the sauce. Continue cooking until the sauce thickens and most of the tomatoes burst. You may need to add reserved pasta water, depending on how juicy the tomatoes are.

3. Whole canned tomatoes should be strained before being added to the pan in step 6. A food mill comes in handy for puréeing the tomatoes. First allow them to drain in the food mill. Discard the excess watery juice the tomatoes are packed in before turning the crank. Use the medium blade. The resulting purée will look quite thin, but it will reduce quickly over a high heat. Chopped tomatoes in juice will also produce good results. Experiment to see what you like best.

4. Add your pasta to the water one portion at a time: one portion of spaghetti (4 ounces) is about as much as you can hold between the joint of your thumb and the first joint of your index finger. It's important to stir the pasta frequently as it begins to boil to keep it from sticking together; stir occasionally after that. Begin cooking pasta right before starting the sauce.

Spaghetti and tomato sauce start simultaneously in separate pots but come together for the final minutes of cooking. Each strand becomes evenly coated and colored, and imbued with the sauce's lovely flavor.

5. Heat a 12-inch sauté pan over medium heat. Add the extra-virgin olive oil to the pan. Heat slowly so that the oil does not lose its green hue. Add the pieces of garlic, and cook, stirring until lightly golden. Add the crushed red-pepper flakes and the salt to the oil; cook until garlic is medium brown. Do not burn the garlic.

6. Tilt the pan away from you to avoid spattering; add the tomatoes, along with reserved juices, to the pan. Cook the mixture over high heat, swirling occasionally, until tomatoes break down and become saucelike.

7. While the tomatoes continue to cook in the sauté pan, drain the pasta, reserving some of the cooking water and shaking the colander a few times. Do not rinse the pasta.

8. Slide pasta into the pan with the tomato sauce; toss with tongs to coat. If it gets too dry, add some reserved pasta water. Cook until sauce clings to pasta. Add torn basil leaves to pan, and cook. Divide the pasta mixture among two or four heated bowls; finish with a grating of cheese, if desired.

Perfect Pizza

¼ teaspoon sugar

1 package dry yeast
(2¼ teaspoons)

2¾ to 3¼ cups all-purpose
unbleached flour

1 teaspoon salt

1½ tablespoons olive oil, plus
more for oiling the bowl
Coarse-grain yellow
cornmeal, for dusting
Pizza Sauce (recipe follows)

1 pound fresh mozzarella cheese,
thinly sliced
Fresh thyme (optional), chopped
Crushed red-pepper flakes
(optional)

For illustrated instructions, see Pizza 101 on page 68. If you have trouble stretching the dough with your fists, use a rolling pin to roll it out; just be sure to stretch the inside slightly so it is thin.   **makes two 12-inch round pizzas**

1. Heat oven to 500°, with a 16-inch-diameter pizza stone placed on lowest shelf, for at least 30 minutes. Pour 1 cup warm water (about 110°) into a small bowl. Add the sugar, and sprinkle in the yeast. Using a fork, stir the mixture until the yeast is dissolved and water has turned a tan color. Let yeast stand until foamy, about 5 minutes. In a food processor, use blade to combine the 2¾ cups flour and salt, and pulse 3 to 4 times. Add yeast mixture and 1½ tablespoons olive oil. Pulse until the dough comes together, adding more flour as needed until dough is smooth, not tacky, when squeezed. Transfer to a clean surface; knead four or five turns into a ball.

2. Brush the inside of a medium bowl with oil, and place dough in the bowl, smooth-side up. Cover tightly with plastic wrap, and place in a warm spot until doubled in size, about 40 minutes. Remove wrap, and punch down dough with your fist. Fold dough back onto itself four or five times. Turn dough over, folded-side down, cover with plastic wrap, and return to the warm spot to rise again until the dough has doubled in size, about 30 minutes.

3. Punch down the dough, and transfer to a clean surface. Using a sharp knife, divide dough in half, and knead each half four or five turns into a ball. Place one of the dough balls back in the oiled bowl, and cover with plastic wrap. Lightly flour a clean surface, place the remaining dough ball on top, pat into a flattened circle, cover lightly with wrap, and let rest 5 minutes. Using your fingers, flatten and push the dough evenly out from the center until it measures 7 to 8 inches in diameter. Do not press the dough all the way to edges. Leave a slightly raised border, about ½ inch wide, around pizza dough.

4. Sprinkle cornmeal over the surface of a pizza peel. Set aside. Lift the dough off the surface, and center it on top of your fists. Hold your fists 1 to 2 inches apart. Begin to rotate and stretch the dough, opening your fists until they are 6 to 8 inches apart and the dough is several inches larger. Place your fists under the inside of the outer edge, and continue to stretch the dough a little at a time until it reaches about 12 inches in diameter.

5. Arrange the pizza dough into a circle on top of the cornmeal-dusted peel. Pour 9 tablespoons of the pizza sauce onto the dough. Using the back of a tablespoon, evenly spread the sauce, leaving a half-inch border of dough uncovered. Arrange half of the mozzarella slices on top of the sauce.

6. Lift the pizza peel and, using a slight jerking motion, slide the pizza about 1 inch back and forth on the peel to loosen it. Place the front tip of the peel on the back side of the stone. Slide the pizza off the peel. Bake until the crust is golden brown and crisp on the edges and the bottom, 12 to 18 minutes, turning the pizza halfway through baking. Using tongs, lift the edge of the pizza, and slide the peel all the way under to remove it from the oven. Sprinkle with thyme and pepper flakes, if desired. Using a pizza wheel, slice the pizza into eight pieces, and serve immediately. While first pizza is baking, shape and assemble a second pizza using remaining dough and ingredients. Repeat process, and serve.

2 tablespoons olive oil

1 twenty-eight-ounce can
whole Italian peeled plum
tomatoes

¾ teaspoon dried oregano

1½ teaspoons salt

⅛ teaspoon freshly ground pepper

Pizza Sauce   **makes enough for 2 pizzas**

1. Pour the olive oil into a large skillet. Place over medium heat. Using your hands, squeeze the tomatoes to crush them. Add to the olive oil, along with the remaining ingredients. Cook over medium-low heat, breaking up tomatoes with a wooden spoon, until the sauce is thick, 40 to 50 minutes.

2. Pass sauce through a food mill, discard the seeds, and let cool. May be made up to 1 week ahead and kept, refrigerated, in an airtight container.

From blazing hot baking stone to cutting board to plate in a matter of minutes, homemade pizza is always the best. Cut into wedges while the mozzarella and sauce are still fragrant and bubbling, and the thin crust is still crackling. Sprinkle with chopped fresh thyme and crushed red-pepper flakes to taste, and serve. To help cool the first hot bites, make sure a glass of cold beer is standing by.

Pizza 101

Italophiles, here's how you do it. Start by making your dough (*pasta*). Let the dough rise (*falla lievitare*), punch it down (*sgonfiala*), and toss it into the air (*gettata in aria*). Pull and stretch the dough until it becomes a thin elastic circle. Brush tomato sauce over the surface of the dough, swishing back and forth as if painting a vast fresco. Imported canned tomatoes will make a fine sauce. In fact, depending on the season, they are preferable to the pale approximation you could make with supermarket tomatoes. Scatter cheese (*il formaggio*), basil (*il basilico*), and one or two other carefully selected ingredients over the sauce. After scattering the mozzarella, clap your hands together right above the pizza. Half blessing and half suggestion, it is a hint to the pizza to behave. Place it in a very hot oven (*il forno*), close the door, and wait for it to emerge—thin, golden, hot, and bubbly. *Perfetto.*

1. Pulse the salt and flour in the bowl of a food processor. Add the proofed yeast and olive oil; process until the dough is smooth and not tacky to the touch. This means it has "come together," and formed one heavy ball, which is what you want.

2. Shape the dough into a round. Set in a bowl that's been brushed with olive oil. Cover with plastic wrap to rise in a warm spot. The dough will rise because the yeast, which eats the sugars and starches in the flour, releases alcohol and carbon dioxide, causing the dough to bubble and get full and fat. The term until "doubled in size" is a visual rule of thumb, indicating that the dough is ready.

3. Punch back the dough, and let it rise again. Pushing down the dough releases the gases and redistributes the sugars and starches that yeast lives on. It is also a good way to release all of your aggressions.

4. Transfer the dough to a work surface, cut in half, and gently knead each half into a ball. Let dough rest.

A few tools turn your kitchen into a real pizzeria—a food processor, a wooden peel, and a ceramic stone. But it's still your hands that make homemade pizza perfect.

5. On a floured surface, begin to form the pizza by pressing the dough out into a flat circle. Pressing from the center, form a circle that is about 7 to 8 inches in diameter with a raised border around the edge.

6. Lift the dough off the surface. Place it centered on top of your fists. Rotate and stretch the dough, pulling your fists apart until dough is several inches larger. Shift your fists away from the center of dough (if it gets too stretched in that area, it will tear) toward but not touching the border, so the dough now drapes over your fists; pull and stretch the dough out into a thin circle, about 12 inches in diameter, making sure to maintain the slightly raised border. The dough will drape down over your forearms.

7. Transfer the dough to a pizza peel, dusted with cornmeal to prevent sticking. Spoon a thin, even coat of tomato sauce over the dough, staying inside the dough border.

8. Arrange thin slices of mozzarella (and other toppings of your choice), and transfer the pizza onto the stone. Tilt the peel, and slide the pizza off it, centering it on the stone. When pizza is finished baking, use the peel to remove it from the oven. Slide the peel under the pizza, and lift the baked pizza up and out of the oven.

All-American Meat Loaf

Ingredients

- 3 slices white bread
- 1 large carrot, peeled and cut into ¼-inch-thick rounds
- 1 rib celery, cut into ½-inch pieces
- ½ medium yellow onion, roughly chopped
- 2 cloves garlic, smashed
- ½ cup fresh flat-leaf parsley leaves, loosely packed
- ½ cup plus 3 tablespoons ketchup
- 4½ teaspoons dry mustard
- 8 ounces ground pork
- 8 ounces ground veal
- 8 ounces ground beef
- 2 large eggs, beaten
- 2 teaspoons salt
- 1 teaspoon freshly ground pepper
- 1 teaspoon Tabasco, or to taste
- ½ teaspoon chopped rosemary, plus more needles for sprinkling
- 2 tablespoons dark-brown sugar
- 1 tablespoon olive oil
- 1 small red onion, cut into ¼-inch-thick rings

Cooking the free-form loaf on a wire baking rack allows the meat fats to drain off and an evenly glazed crust to form. Do not substitute dried bread crumbs for homemade; they will make your meat loaf rubbery. **serves 6**

1. Heat oven to 400°. Remove the crusts from the bread. Place slices in the bowl of a food processor. Process until fine crumbs form, about 10 seconds. Transfer bread crumbs to a large mixing bowl. Place the carrot, celery, yellow onion, garlic, and parsley in the bowl of the food processor. Process until vegetables are minced, about 30 seconds, stopping to scrape down the sides of the bowl once or twice. Transfer the vegetable mixture to the bowl with the bread crumbs. Add ½ cup ketchup, 2 teaspoons dry mustard, the pork, veal, beef, eggs, salt, pepper, Tabasco, and rosemary. Using your hands, knead ingredients until thoroughly combined, about 1 minute. Do not overknead; it will result in a heavy and dense loaf: The texture should be wet, but tight enough to hold a free-form shape.

2. Set a fine-mesh baking rack in an 11-by-17-inch baking pan. Cut a 5-by-11-inch piece of parchment paper, and place over center of rack to prevent meat loaf from falling through. Using your hands, form an elongated loaf covering the parchment.

3. Place the remaining 3 tablespoons ketchup, remaining 2½ teaspoons mustard, and the brown sugar in a bowl. Mix until smooth. Using a pastry brush, generously brush the glaze over the loaf. Place the oil in a medium saucepan set over high heat. When oil is smoking, add the red onion. Cook, stirring occasionally, until onion is soft and golden in places, about 10 minutes. Add 3 tablespoons water, and cook, stirring, until most of the water has evaporated. Transfer the onion to a bowl to cool slightly, then sprinkle onion over the meat loaf.

4. Bake the meat loaf 30 minutes, then sprinkle rosemary needles on top. Continue baking loaf until an instant-read thermometer inserted into the center of the loaf registers 160°, about 25 minutes more. Let meat loaf cool on rack about 15 minutes, and serve.

There's a lot more to great meat loaf than meets the eye. This one is a moist and savory mix of ground beef, pork, and veal; aromatic touches of minced carrot, onion, celery, garlic, and rosemary; spicy mustard and Tabasco; and fresh eggs and bread crumbs for a light firm texture. And that's just the inside: Before baking, the loaf is coated with a glaze of ketchup, mustard, and brown sugar, and then smothered with sautéed onions. Buttery mashed potatoes are a must with meat loaf—splash both generously with thick pan gravy.

Classic Cheeseburger

2 pounds ground beef, preferably chuck

2 teaspoons salt

1/4 teaspoon freshly ground pepper

3 ounces cheddar or Monterey Jack cheese, sliced 1/4-inch thick

4 hamburger buns

2 tomatoes (12 ounces), sliced

8 Bibb lettuce leaves (1 small head)

1 small red onion, sliced

These burgers are big—the recipe makes four hefty half-pounders. You can form the meat into smaller patties if you wish, and reduce the grilling time slightly. Of course, feel free to omit the cheese. **serves 4**

1. Heat a grill or grill pan to medium high. Season the meat with salt and pepper, mix very lightly, and shape into four patties. Grill hamburgers 4 to 6 minutes per side for rare and 9 to 11 minutes for well done. If making cheeseburgers, lay the cheese slices on top of the hamburgers after they have been flipped.

2. Serve immediately on buns (toasted, if desired), topped with tomatoes, lettuce, and onion slices.

Turkey Burger With Caramelized Onions

1 tablespoon unsalted butter

1 tablespoon olive oil, plus more for buns

2 large onions (about 1 3/4 pounds), sliced into 1/4-inch rounds

1 teaspoon sugar

2 teaspoons salt

3/4 teaspoon freshly ground pepper

2 teaspoons fresh thyme leaves or 1 teaspoon dried thyme (optional)

1 1/2 pounds ground turkey

1 medium shallot, peeled and finely minced

2 scallions, white parts only, minced

1 teaspoon Tabasco sauce

2 teaspoons Worcestershire sauce

4 whole grain or white hamburger buns

Sliced tomato, for garnish

Lettuce, for garnish

If the burgers brown too quickly, cover them with a heat-proof metal bowl. This will help them to cook them to cook more quickly on the inside. Use tongs or a heavy potholder to remove the hot bowl from the grill. **serves 4**

1. To make the caramelized onions, heat the butter and 1 tablespoon oil in a large skillet over medium-low heat. Add the onions, cover, and cook until they begin to soften, stirring occasionally, about 10 minutes. Add the sugar, 1/2 teaspoon salt, and 1/4 teaspoon pepper, and raise heat slightly. Cook, uncovered, until the onions are golden brown, stirring occasionally, 25 to 30 minutes. Stir in thyme, and set aside.

2. Meanwhile, combine turkey, shallot, scallions, Tabasco, Worcestershire, remaining 1 1/2 teaspoons salt, and 1/2 teaspoon pepper in a large bowl; mix very lightly to combine.

3. Heat a grill or grill pan to medium high. Form four equal patties and cook them through, about 7 minutes per side on the grill, or 8 minutes on the grill pan.

4. To toast the buns, brush the cut sides lightly with olive oil, and toast cut-side-down on the grill, until lightly golden, 20 to 30 seconds. Top burgers with the caramelized onions, and garnish with slices of tomato and lettuce leaves. Serve.

what to put on your hamburger

- Creamy, melting cheese: cheddar, Swiss, mozzarella, blue cheese, or Gorgonzola
- Onion: raw, grilled, or caramelized; red, white, or sweet
- Thick slices of beefsteak tomato
- Pickles: dill, kosher, garlic-cured, or sweet
- Sliced mushrooms sautéed with Marsala wine
- Chopped chipotles in adobo sauce
- Roasted garlic

- Asian chili-garlic paste
- Grilled eggplant
- Pickled jalapeños
- A slice of pickled green tomato
- Hummus
- Roasted yellow and red peppers
- Good-quality prepared salsa
- Good-quality prepared mango chutney

This Turkey Burger With Caramelized Onions (left) has minced shallots, thyme, and Worcestershire mixed in the meat, and gets piled with caramelized onions after it's grilled. Make a bed of Bibb lettuce and sliced tomato on a whole-grain roll, and serve with potato chips and a simple sweet-and-sour slaw of red cabbage. A Classic Cheeseburger (below) is crusty and juicy under a melted slice of Monterey Jack or cheddar cheese. Set it on a lightly grilled kaiser roll slathered with mayo and grainy mustard and topped with multiple layers of crisp red onion, tomato slices, and Bibb lettuce.

Roast Chicken 101

1 six-pound roasting chicken

2 tablespoons unsalted butter
  Salt and freshly ground pepper

2 medium onions, peeled and
  sliced crosswise ½ inch thick

1 lemon

3 large cloves garlic, peeled

4 sprigs fresh thyme

8 new potatoes, cut in half

4 large carrots, halved lengthwise
  and quartered

1 tablespoon olive oil

1 cup Chicken Stock (recipe,
  page 56), or canned

Handling raw chicken and other poultry requires some precautions: Discard all paper towels used to dry the chicken, and wash all tools, work surfaces, and your hands with warm soapy water immediately. Make sure the chicken is fully cooked. Pierce the skin where the thigh meets the body, and check that the juices are clear, with no pink color. And, if you can, check the internal temperature of the meat with an instant-read thermometer. See illustrated instructions, page 76.　　**serves 4**

1. Let the chicken and 1 tablespoon butter stand at room temperature for 30 minutes. Heat oven to 425°. Remove and discard the plastic pop-up timer from the chicken if there is one. Remove the giblets and excess fat from the chicken cavity. Rinse the chicken inside and out under cold running water. Dry the chicken thoroughly with paper towels. Tuck the wing tips under the body. Sprinkle the cavity of the chicken liberally with salt and pepper, and set aside.

2. In the center of a heavy-duty roasting pan, place onion slices in two rows, touching.

3. Place the palm of your hand on top of the lemon and, pressing down, roll back and forth several times. Pierce the entire surface of the lemon with a fork. Using the side of a large knife, gently press on the garlic cloves to open slightly. Insert garlic cloves, thyme sprigs, and lemon into cavity. Place chicken in pan, on onion slices. Cut about eighteen inches of kitchen twine, bring chicken legs forward, cross them, and tie together.

4. Spread the softened butter over entire surface of the chicken, and sprinkle liberally with salt and pepper. Place in the oven, and roast for 15 minutes. Meanwhile, in a medium bowl toss together the potatoes, carrots, and oil, and season with salt and pepper. Remove pan from the oven, and scatter potatoes and carrots around the chicken. Return pan to the oven, and continue roasting the chicken until the skin is deep golden brown and crisp and the juices run clear when pierced, 45 minutes to 1 hour 15 minutes more. When the chicken seems done, insert an instant-read thermometer into the breast, then the thigh. The breast temperature should read 180° and the thigh 190°.

5. Remove the chicken from oven, and transfer to a cutting board with a well. Let the chicken stand 10 to 15 minutes so the juices settle. Meanwhile, transfer the potatoes and carrots to a serving platter. Pour the pan drippings into a shallow bowl or fat separator, and leave the onions in the pan. Leave any brown baked-on bits in the bottom of the roasting pan, and remove and discard any blackened bits. Using a large spoon or fat separator, skim off and discard as much fat as possible. Pour the remaining drippings and the juices that have collected under the resting chicken back into the roasting pan. Place on the stove over medium-high heat to cook, about 1 minute. Add the chicken stock, raise heat to high, and, using a wooden spoon, stir up and combine the brown bits with the stock until the liquid is reduced by half, about 4 minutes. Strain the gravy into a small bowl, pressing on the onions to extract any liquid. Discard onion, and stir in the remaining tablespoon of cold butter until melted and incorporated. Untie the legs, and remove and discard the garlic, thyme, and lemon. Carve, and serve with gravy and vegetables on the side.

A plump, golden roasted chicken fills the house with fragrance—and anticipation—as it awaits carving. Here, fresh herbs, lemon, and other seasonings infuse the flesh, and butter crisps the skin. Present on a platter surrounded by roasted potatoes and carrots; serve the gravy you've made from the pan juices on the side.

How to Roast a Chicken

The ideal roast chicken — golden brown and gleaming, tender and juicy — engages all of the senses. The crackle of the chicken as it cooks and the wondrous aroma that perfumes the kitchen evoke different, very personal feelings in everybody. While the perfect roast chicken may seem like simplicity itself, achieving the proper levels of crispness, flavor, color, and moisture are questions that have long challenged cooks at all levels. The basic elements of the chicken seem to be at war with one another, with the leaner, more tender, white breast meat needing less cooking than the richer, fattier dark meat of the leg. This recipe does not require any turning or basting. Tying the legs of the chicken together helps the meat to cook evenly, and spreading butter over the entire surface of the chicken before cooking ensures a delectable crispness and an appetizing golden-brown color.

  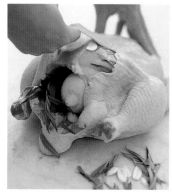 

1. To ensure even cooking, let the chicken stand at room temperature for 30 minutes. If the chicken comes with a plastic pop-up thermometer, discard it; the readings are often inaccurate. After rinsing the chicken inside and out with water, dry thoroughly. Tuck the tips of the wings under the bottom to keep them from burning.

2. Place onions in rows in a roasting pan to form a bed for the chicken. The onions will flavor the chicken and the pan juices that form the base of the gravy. They also provide a rack for the chicken, keeping it out of the juice, and prevent the skin from sticking to the pan. Put garlic, thyme, and lemon inside the chicken's cavity. The chicken will absorb the aromas and flavors as it cooks.

3. In a variation of step two, gently loosen the skin from both sides of the breast without tearing the skin. Place 2 cloves of garlic, thinly sliced, and 2 sprigs of tarragon between the meat and skin to further amplify the flavors (substitute 2 sprigs of tarragon for the thyme in the cavity).

4. Place chicken on onions breast-side up. Bring legs forward, cross them, and tie them together with kitchen twine. Tying the legs is much simpler than trussing the bird, which requires tying the body. Spread butter over the surface of the chicken. Smearing the bird with butter ensures that the chicken will brown evenly. Sprinkle with salt and pepper.

Treat your chicken royally: Put lemon and fresh thyme inside and garlic and tarragon under the breast skin. Give it a rub with soft butter, and set it on an aromatic bed of onion slices before roasting.

5. Cook the chicken; when ready, the skin will be crisp and golden brown, and the juices should run clear. To be sure the chicken is finished cooking, check the internal temperature of the breasts and the thighs with an instant-read thermometer. Be careful that you don't touch any of the bones with the thermometer. Bones conduct heat and will give a false reading.

6. When the chicken is finished cooking, transfer it to a cutting board, and let the chicken stand. The juices, which rise to the surface when cooking, will settle and redistribute evenly throughout the chicken. Pour the pan drippings into a fat separator, leaving the onions in the pan; discard as much of the fat as possible.

7. This gravy is easy to make and delicious: Pour the defatted drippings, along with any juices that have collected on the cutting board, back into the pan. Place the pan on the stove; cook for about 1 minute. Add chicken stock. Over high heat, stir up any baked-on brown bits so they combine with the stock; these brown bits add flavor to the gravy. Cook until the liquid is reduced by half.

8. Strain the gravy. Stir in remaining butter until it is fully incorporated. To carve: Untie the legs. Remove lemon, garlic, and herbs from cavity; discard. Place chicken on a serving platter breast-side up. Use a large fork to pull one of the legs away from the body, then use a sharp knife to sever the joint that connects the leg to the body. Cut the thigh from the drumstick at the second joint. To remove breasts, cut straight down between them, following the contour of the rib cage, until you hit the wishbone. Cut through the joint where it meets the breastbone, and serve.

Fried Chicken

6 cups buttermilk

¼ cup plus 5 teaspoons salt

⅓ cup Tabasco (optional)

2 two- to three-pound chickens, each cut into 8 pieces for frying

3 cups all-purpose flour

1 tablespoon freshly ground black pepper

1½ teaspoons ground cayenne pepper

2 pounds vegetable shortening

6 tablespoons bacon drippings (optional)

Fried chicken gets the best flavor from long marinating and a well-seasoned coating mix. A small amount of bacon grease added to the vegetable shortening lends extra taste, too. Fry dark meat pieces in a separate batch from the white breast and wing pieces, as they have different cooking times. A deep-frying thermometer is the only reliable way to check the temperature of the hot shortening—if you like fried chicken, you should have one.   **serves 8**

1. Combine the buttermilk, ¼ cup salt, and Tabasco, if using, in a bowl or a large, airtight container. Add the chicken pieces, turning to coat in the liquid. Cover, and refrigerate for at least 2 hours or overnight.

2. Combine the flour, remaining 5 teaspoons salt, and black and cayenne peppers in a large brown paper bag. Shake vigorously.

3. One at a time, place the chicken pieces in the bag, and shake to coat. Place coated pieces on a clean plate or tray. Heat the vegetable shortening (and bacon drippings if using) in two 10-inch cast-iron skillets over medium-low heat. Using a frying thermometer to measure temperature, bring shortening to 375°; it should be at a medium, not a rolling, boil. Use tongs to place thighs and drumsticks in skillets. Fry until the coating is dark golden on the bottom, 10 to 14 minutes; then, using tongs, turn chicken over. Cook until the coating is dark golden, another 10 to 14 minutes. An instant-read thermometer inserted into a thigh should register 170°. Drain on a cooling rack or several layered paper towels. Using a slotted spoon, remove any bits of coating left in skillets, and discard. Place breasts and wings in skillets. Cook 10 to 14 minutes on each side. Drain and serve.

"It takes me back to Georgia. It's in my soul.

Both Mama and my grandmother would fix it for

Sunday supper. My grandfather called it 'Gospel Bird.'

I remember cast-iron skillets slick and black like satin, pulling

the wishbone with my mother, and fighting over the

drumsticks with my sister." —VIRGINIA WILLIS, TELEVISION KITCHEN DIRECTOR

The best Fried Chicken gets a buttermilk bath for tenderness and a seasoned-flour coating for lots of crunch and spice. Carry cooled chicken pieces to a picnic in a mesh wire basket, and serve with wedges of watermelon and seasonal salads. On cold days, load the table with chicken pieces while they're still warm from the skillet, with a bowl of mashed potatoes, pan gravy, and cooked greens.

food for gatherings

chapter four

What makes certain foods so comforting?

This deep-dish potpie covers a soul-warming chicken-and-vegetable stew with a rustic, savory pastry crust. Bring it into the dining room right from the oven, with creamy sauce bubbling through the slits in the flaky crust, the escaping aroma signaling to all that dinner is ready.

A potpie is in the oven for dinner, and everybody starts to feel good long before the first bite. As it bakes, the casserole fills the air with the aroma of meat, vegetables, and buttery pastry, and all heads turn expectantly toward the kitchen. The deep dish is brought into the dining room, and eyes open wide. There's plenty for all. Before you take the first bite, you pause a moment, the steam rising to your face, a promise of warmth through and through.

Yet there's more to comfort than this. Our favorite foods connect us with other times and special people, with those who first made them for us, whose presence first made them so pleasurable: the grandmother whose Sunday supper gathered the clan, the father who carefully loaded a spoon and blew on it gently, until it was just cool enough to eat.

The real magic is in the cooking and the sharing. Comfort is a gift we give whenever we feed our family and friends. Here are big, hot, generous dishes—hearty stews and savory potpies brimming with fresh ingredients and delicious flavors, to fill everybody you care about with good feelings and lasting memories.

Sweet Italian spring onions, brussels sprouts, fennel, carrots, and parsnips are braised in a light tomato sauce with hot Italian sausage and aromatic herbs in Savory Fall Stew. It is slow-cooked and spooned over Baked Sage and Saffron Risotto.

Black Bean and Tomato Chili

1¾ cups dried black beans

3 large or 4 small dried guajillo chiles

2 tablespoons olive oil

2 medium onions, finely chopped

8 cloves garlic, minced

4 teaspoons ground cumin

1¾ cups Chicken Stock (recipe, page 56), or canned

2 pounds assorted ripe tomatoes, seeded and cut into 1-inch chunks

½ cup fresh basil leaves, roughly chopped

1½ teaspoons salt

¼ teaspoon freshly ground pepper

2 tablespoons balsamic vinegar

Serve this pungent chili, infused with raw and cooked garlic, over cooked rice seasoned with turmeric.   **serves 6**

1. Soak the black beans in 3 cups water overnight. (Or place beans in a medium saucepan, and cover with 2 inches of water. Place lid on pan, and bring to a boil. Remove from heat, and let sit for 1 hour.) Drain the beans in a colander, and set aside.

2. Set a small skillet over high heat. Place the chiles in the pan; toast on both sides until browned and puffed, about 1 minute. Transfer chiles to a small bowl, and cover with ⅔ cup hot water. Let sit 10 minutes. Cut the chiles in half, and remove the seeds and stems. Transfer the flesh, along with the poaching liquid, to the bowl of a food processor. Process until a purée forms.

3. Place a medium saucepan over medium heat. Add the olive oil, and let warm. Add the onions, three-quarters of the minced garlic, and the cumin. Cover, and cook until softened and slightly browned, about 15 minutes. Add the chile purée, and cook 2 minutes more. Add the stock and the reserved black beans. Cover, and cook until the beans are soft, about 1½ hours. If the beans seem dry, add another ½ cup hot water.

4. In a large bowl, toss together the tomatoes, remaining minced garlic, basil, salt, pepper, and vinegar. Let sit 5 minutes. Stir half of the tomato mixture into the beans. Cover, and simmer 1 minute more.

5. Divide the chili among six bowls. Top with remaining tomato mixture, and serve.

Savory Fall Stew

2 tablespoons olive oil

12 ounces hot Italian sausage, cut into small chunks

12 cipollini onions (pearl onions can be substituted), peeled

1½ cups crushed tomatoes

3 cups Chicken Stock (recipe, page 56), or canned

1 small bundle of fresh herbs, such as rosemary, thyme, or oregano

1 2½-pound butternut squash, peeled, seeded, and cut into 1-inch chunks

3 carrots, peeled and cut into ½-inch pieces

3 parsnips, peeled and cut into 2-inch-long sticks

1 fennel bulb, trimmed and cut into ¼-inch-thick slices

12 brussels sprouts, trimmed and cut in half

2 teaspoons salt

⅛ teaspoon freshly ground pepper

You can make this a vegetarian dish simply by omitting the sausage and the first step in the instructions. Once the vegetables are cleaned and cut, this stew is easy to make: Everything just simmers on the stove. The stew may be prepared two days ahead and refrigerated. Serve it with a rice dish such as Baked Sage and Saffron Risotto (recipe, page 110) or plain white rice.   **serves 4**

1. Heat the oil in a saucepan over medium heat. Add the sausage, and cook, stirring until it breaks into small pieces and is no longer pink, about 10 minutes. Remove the sausage with a slotted spoon, and set aside.

2. Pour off all but 2 tablespoons rendered fat, and discard. Raise heat to medium high, add the onions, and cook, stirring, until golden, 5 to 6 minutes. Add the tomatoes, stock, and herbs; simmer over medium heat until the liquid starts to thicken, 20 to 25 minutes. Add the sausage, squash, carrots, parsnips, and fennel; cover, and simmer until vegetables are tender, about 10 minutes. Add brussels sprouts, and cook, covered, about 5 minutes more. Remove cover, and cook, stirring occasionally, until liquid thickens, 10 to 15 minutes more. Season with salt and pepper, and serve.

Chunky Vegetable Potpie

½ butternut squash, peeled and
cut into ¾-inch cubes (about
8 ounces)

1 small head celeriac, peeled and
cut into ½-inch cubes

2 medium carrots, peeled and cut
into thick matchsticks

½ cup white cauliflower florets

½ cup green cauliflower florets

8 ounces brussels sprouts, cleaned
and trimmed, sliced lengthwise
if large

1 medium beet, peeled and cut into
¼-inch pieces

1 small turnip or 2 parsnips, peeled
and cut into thick 1-inch-long
matchsticks

¼ cup olive oil

¾ teaspoon salt

⅛ teaspoon freshly ground pepper

3 cloves garlic, minced

2 medium shallots, minced

½ cup dry white wine

1½ cups canned vegetable broth

1 cup plus 2 tablespoons
all-purpose flour

2 teaspoons baking powder

2 tablespoons plus 2 teaspoons
chopped fresh tarragon

3 tablespoons unsalted butter

½ cup milk

2 tablespoons freshly grated
Parmesan cheese

1 medium zucchini, cut into 1-inch-
long thick matchsticks

Use any combination of white, purple, or green cauliflower in this recipe. Chicken Stock (recipe, page 56) may be used in place of vegetable broth. **serves 6**

1. Heat oven to 425°. Place the squash, celeriac, carrots, white and green cauliflower, brussels sprouts, beet, and turnip or parsnips in a large roasting pan. Toss with 2 tablespoons olive oil, ½ teaspoon salt, and ⅛ teaspoon pepper. Roast for 35 to 40 minutes, stirring twice during the cooking. Remove, and reduce oven to 375°.

2. Heat remaining 2 tablespoons olive oil in a medium skillet over medium heat. Add garlic and shallots; sauté until soft, about 5 minutes. Raise heat to high, and add wine. Let wine reduce by half, 1 to 2 minutes. Add vegetable broth, and simmer over medium-high heat for 5 minutes. Set aside.

3. Combine 1 cup flour, baking powder, remaining ¼ teaspoon salt, and 2 teaspoons tarragon in the bowl of a food processor. Pulse in the butter until the mixture resembles coarse meal. Add the milk and the Parmesan, and process until combined. Set biscuit dough aside.

4. Transfer the vegetable mixture to a large bowl. Add the zucchini, remaining 2 tablespoons flour, and 2 tablespoons tarragon; toss to combine. Stir in the broth.

5. Transfer to a shallow dish. Bake for 15 minutes. Remove mixture from the oven, and drop heaping tablespoons of biscuit dough over the vegetables, leaving some vegetables exposed. Place the dish on a baking sheet to catch any drips, and bake until the biscuits are golden, about 25 minutes. Serve potpie hot; spoon out portions with vegetables and biscuits for each serving.

A gardenful of roasted vegetables, including squash, cauliflower, brussels sprouts, beets and turnips, fill this potpie. The vegetables are moistened with white-wine sauce, topped with drop-biscuit dough, and baked in a deep dish.

White Bean and Vegetable Stew

12 ounces dried cannellini or white beans (1¾ cups)

1 tablespoon whole black peppercorns

2 dried bay leaves

1 small onion (about 4 ounces), thickly sliced

1 tablespoon salt, plus more to taste

2 lemons

12 baby artichokes (about 1¾ pounds)

1 large bunch fresh basil (4 cups loosely packed leaves)

6 tablespoons olive oil

4 large leeks (2 pounds), white and light-green parts only

2 teaspoons minced garlic (from 2 large cloves)

¼ teaspoon freshly ground pepper, plus more to taste

1 cup dry white wine

3 small heads radicchio (about 1 pound)

This vegetarian stew can be made up to a day in advance and reheated—just add the radicchio and the basil purée right before you reheat the stew.   **serves 6 to 8**

1. Pick over beans, discarding any stones or broken beans, and rinse. Place in a large saucepan, cover with cold water by 2 inches, and bring to a strong boil. Remove from heat, and let stand 1 hour, covered. (Alternatively, the beans can be placed in a bowl, covered with 2 inches of cold water, and soaked overnight.)

2. Drain the beans, place them in the saucepan, and add enough cold water to cover by 2 inches. Tie the peppercorns in a small piece of cheesecloth, and add to beans along with the bay leaves and onion slices. Return the mixture to heat, bring to a boil, and reduce heat to medium low. Simmer until the beans are very tender, 35 to 40 minutes, adding 1 teaspoon salt about 10 minutes before beans are finished cooking. Remove from heat, set aside, and let the beans cool in their liquid. They can be cooked and refrigerated in their liquid up to two days in advance.

3. Meanwhile, fill a large bowl with cold water. Cut lemons in half, squeeze juice into water, and add lemon halves. Trim about ½ inch from the tips of the artichokes, and pull off tough outer leaves. Trim stems to ½ inch, and trim off dark green outer layer of stem. Slice artichokes in half lengthwise if small or in quarters if large. Use a small sharp knife to remove the purple choke from artichokes— if the choke is not purple, it is not necessary to remove it. Place prepared artichokes in the bowl of lemon water. Set aside.

4. Remove basil leaves from stems, discard stems, and wash thoroughly. Drain and lay leaves out on paper towels, blotting away as much water as possible. Place basil in the bowl of a food processor, add 4 tablespoons olive oil, and process until smooth, about 2 minutes. Transfer purée to a small bowl, cover immediately with plastic wrap to prevent discoloration, and refrigerate until needed.

5. Cut leeks into ½-inch rounds, and place in a large bowl of cold water. Let sit for 5 to 10 minutes to rid them of any dirt and sand. Lift out of the water, and drain in a colander.

6. Heat remaining 2 tablespoons olive oil in a Dutch oven or large saucepan over medium heat. Add leeks, garlic, 1 teaspoon salt, and ⅛ teaspoon pepper, and cook until fragrant and tender, stirring frequently, about 10 minutes. Drain artichokes, discarding the liquid and lemons, and add to the leeks along with the wine. Cover and cook until artichokes begin to become tender, about 15 minutes. Uncover and cook until liquid evaporates and artichokes are tender, about 5 minutes more.

7. Meanwhile, cut radicchio heads into 1-inch wedges without removing the core; it will hold the leaves together. Drain cooked beans, reserving cooking liquid. Remove and discard bay leaves, onion slices, and peppercorns. Add beans, 2 cups of the cooking liquid, remaining 1 teaspoon salt, and ⅛ teaspoon pepper to the leeks and artichokes. Cook until beans are heated through and liquid has thickened, about 15 minutes. Stir in the radicchio wedges, and cook until wilted, about 5 minutes. Adjust seasoning with salt and pepper, if necessary. Stir in 3 tablespoons of the basil purée. Serve immediately with the remaining basil purée on the side.

Chicken Potpie

1 three- to four-pound chicken

4 cups Chicken Stock (recipe, page 56), or canned

1 large yellow onion, split in half

2 dried bay leaves

½ teaspoon whole black peppercorns

1 small bunch fresh thyme

1 rib celery, cut into thirds

1 cup plus 5 tablespoons all-purpose flour

2¼ teaspoons salt

8 tablespoons (1 stick) plus 7 tablespoons unsalted butter

2 large egg yolks

9 ounces red potatoes, scrubbed and cut into ½-inch pieces

12 pearl onions, peeled and cut lengthwise if large

1 medium leek, white and light-green parts only, sliced into ¼-inch-thick rounds and washed

2 medium carrots, peeled and sliced into ¼-inch-thick rounds

6 ounces button mushrooms, quartered if large

1 cup milk

2 tablespoons chopped fresh flat-leaf parsley

Zest of 1 lemon

½ teaspoon freshly ground pepper

1 tablespoon heavy cream

Topping a potpie is easy when you use your rolling pin to set the pastry crust over the filled baking dish. Be sure to chill the dough before and after rolling it out, then curl it around the pin and unfurl to cover the pie. Tuck the overlapping edges of pastry inside the dish to create a thick, rustic rim of crust. **serves 6**

1. Combine the chicken, chicken stock, yellow onion, bay leaves, peppercorns, 3 thyme sprigs, and celery in a stockpot, and add enough water just to cover the chicken. Bring the stock to a boil, reduce heat, and simmer, uncovered, for 1 hour.

2. Pick enough thyme leaves to make 3 tablespoons. Combine 1 cup flour, ¼ teaspoon salt, and 1 tablespoon thyme leaves in the bowl of a food processor, and set remaining 2 tablespoons thyme aside. Add 10 tablespoons chilled butter cut into small pieces, and pulse until mixture resembles coarse meal. While the food processor is running, add 3 tablespoons ice water and 1 egg yolk, and process until the dough holds together. Turn dough onto plastic wrap, flatten into circle, and wrap well; refrigerate at least 1 hour.

3. Drain the chicken, and reserve the stock. Remove the skin from the chicken, and remove all the chicken from the carcass. Shred the chicken into bite-size strips, and set aside. Strain the stock, and set aside 2 cups. Reserve the remaining stock for another use.

4. Heat oven to 375°. Melt the remaining 5 tablespoons of butter in a large sauté pan over medium-high heat. Add the red potatoes and pearl onions, and cook, stirring occasionally, 4 to 5 minutes, until the potatoes begin to turn golden. Add the leeks, carrots, and mushrooms, and cook 4 to 5 minutes more. Add the remaining 5 tablespoons flour, and cook, stirring, for 1 minute. Stir in reserved chicken stock and milk, and bring to a simmer. Cook until thick and bubbly, stirring constantly, 2 to 3 minutes. Add reserved chicken pieces, parsley, remaining 2 tablespoons thyme, lemon zest, remaining 2 teaspoons salt, and the ground pepper; transfer to a large casserole dish. Set aside.

5. Roll out the dough until it is ¼ inch thick, and transfer to a baking sheet. Allow to chill 15 minutes. Make an egg wash: In a small bowl, whisk together the remaining yolk and heavy cream. Working quickly, place the dough over the top of the chicken mixture, and tuck extra dough around the edges. Cut slits on top to allow steam to escape. Brush with the egg wash, and place on a baking sheet. Bake 35 to 40 minutes, until crust is golden. Serve hot.

Large chunks of tender poached chicken, carrots, potatoes, and mushrooms in a creamy velouté sauce crowned with a flaky butter crust are the hallmarks of a classic Chicken Potpie. Strips of lemon zest in the filling and fresh thyme in the pastry give this pie a unique fragrance and flavor.

Shepherd's Pie

1½ teaspoons unsalted butter, plus
more for topping
2 pounds boneless beef or lamb for
stew
2 medium onions, chopped
2 tablespoons all-purpose flour
2 cups dry red wine
1 cup Homemade Beef Stock (see
recipe, page 37), or canned
Bouquet garni, made with 1 celery
stalk, 1 sprig each of rosemary
and thyme, 2 crumbled bay
leaves, and 1 clove garlic tied in
cheesecloth
4 carrots, peeled and cut into
3-inch lengths
Salt and freshly ground pepper
3 rutabagas (about 3 pounds)
4 russet or Yukon gold potatoes
(about 1¾ pounds)
½ cup hot milk, or as needed
1 tablespoon chopped fresh rosemary

This dish tastes best if the stew is made a day ahead of time; remove and discard any solidified fat before topping with the vegetable purée.   **serves 8 to 10**

1. Over medium heat, heat a wide, heavy-bottomed lidded pan until hot. Melt the butter, and brown meat in two batches. Add the onions; cook until slightly softened, about 5 minutes. Sprinkle the flour over the meat, and cook until well browned, about 5 to 8 minutes, stirring often.

2. Add wine, and bring to a boil, scraping the bottom of the pan to loosen brown bits. Add the stock and bouquet garni, bring to a boil, cover, and cook on low heat for 1½ hours, or until meat is tender. Remove lid after 1 hour; add the carrots, and cook, uncovered, for the last 30 minutes. Season with salt and pepper.

3. Meanwhile, peel rutabagas and potatoes, and cut into chunks. Place in separate saucepans, and cover with cold salted water. Bring to a boil, and simmer until tender, about 30 to 40 minutes for rutabagas and 25 minutes for potatoes. Drain; return to saucepans to dry for a few minutes.

4. Put the rutabagas and the potatoes through a food mill or ricer, or mash by hand. Add butter to taste, and enough hot milk to make a creamy purée. Season to taste with salt and pepper; stir in the chopped rosemary.

5. Heat oven to 350°. Remove bouquet garni, and turn stew into a deep 2-quart baking dish. Top with purée; dot lightly with butter. Bake for 1 hour, or until the top is brown and crusty. Serve hot.

Spicy Seafood Potpie

1 large shallot, minced
½ cup dry white wine
1 tablespoon salt, plus more to taste
12 small mussels (8 ounces),
debearded and scrubbed
2 tablespoons olive oil
2 cloves garlic, minced
1 medium onion, chopped
3 anchovy fillets, finely chopped
1 twenty-eight-ounce can Italian
plum tomatoes
½ teaspoon crushed red-pepper
flakes
1 large egg
1 tablespoon milk
1 sheet frozen puff pastry, thawed
½ yellow bell pepper, diced
1 tablespoon chopped fresh thyme
1 tablespoon chopped fresh parsley
Freshly ground black pepper
8 ounces wild striped bass, skin
removed, cut into 1-inch pieces
5 ounces calamari, cut into rings
8 ounces shrimp, tail on,
peeled and deveined
6 ounces bay scallops

This is really a "faux" potpie, since the pastry is baked separately, but it is elegant nevertheless. Cod or halibut may be used instead of the wild striped bass.   **makes 6 individual pies**

1. Combine the shallot, wine, salt, and ½ cup water in a medium saucepan, and bring to a simmer. Add the mussels, and cook, covered, until the shells are open, about 2 minutes. Remove the mussels from the shell, and set aside, loosely covered. Discard the shells. Strain the cooking liquid through a double layer of damp cheesecloth, and set aside.

2. Heat the oil in a medium straight-sided sauté pan over medium heat. Add the garlic and onion, and cook, until soft, stirring occasionally, about 5 minutes. Add the anchovies; cook another 2 minutes, stirring. Raise heat to medium high; add the tomatoes, breaking them up slightly with the back of a spoon. Add reserved mussel liquid and red-pepper flakes, and cook until the sauce has thickened, about 25 minutes. Transfer the sauce to the bowl of a food processor or blender, and purée until smooth.

3. Heat oven to 425°. Place six 6-ounce ramekins on a baking sheet, and set aside. In a small bowl, combine the egg and milk, and set aside. Lay the puff pastry on a clean surface. Using a round cookie cutter or the rim of a glass, cut out six pastry rounds a bit larger than the rims of the ramekins. Brush pastry with egg wash; place on a parchment-lined baking sheet. Bake until golden brown and puffed, 9 to 12 minutes. Set aside in a warm place.

4. Return sauce to sauté pan; stir in the yellow peppers, thyme, and parsley. Season with salt and pepper. Stir in all the seafood; distribute mixture evenly among ramekins. Place on a baking sheet; bake until juicy and bubbling, 15 to 20 minutes. Place a round of puff pastry on top of each cup, and serve immediately.

Spicy Seafood Potpie (left) is baked and served in individual ramekins, each with airy rounds of puff pastry floating on top of a spicy tomato stew of scallops, shrimp, calamari, mussels, and fish. The pastry tops and sauce can be prepared ahead of time, and the seafood cooked briefly in the oven just before serving. A ragoût of tender chunks of beef and aromatic vegetables (below), slowly braised in red-wine sauce, lies beneath a rich, buttery mash of potatoes and rutabagas in this version of Shepherd's Pie.

"It's all about the crust." —DEBRA PUCHALLA, COPY EDITOR

Spicy aromas rise from this Indian-inspired Curry Chickpea Potpie, a tantalizing fusion of fresh vegetables, earthy legumes, and whole grains. The filling is a blend of broccoli, carrots, cabbage, potatoes, lentils, and chickpeas, infused with garlic, ginger, and curry. A creamy layer of steamed millet forms a crunchy crust when baked. On the side: Cucumber Raita.

Curry Chickpea Potpie

4 tablespoons unsalted butter

1 cup millet

2 large eggs

³/₄ teaspoon salt, plus more for saucepan

2 tablespoons chopped fresh flat-leaf parsley

8 ounces broccoli

1 medium onion, chopped

2 cups shredded green cabbage

2 cloves garlic, minced

1 tablespoon freshly grated ginger

1 tablespoon curry powder

2 large carrots, peeled and cut into ¹/₂-inch dice

8 ounces small white potatoes, quartered

¹/₃ cup red lentils

¹/₂ cup canned chickpeas, drained
Freshly ground pepper
Cucumber Raita (recipe follows)

Serve this potpie with Cucumber Raita, a cooling Indian yogurt sauce.   **serves 6**

1. Boil 2 cups of water. Melt 1 tablespoon of butter in a large skillet over medium-high heat. Add the millet, and sauté until golden brown, 2 to 3 minutes, stirring frequently. Add another tablespoon butter and the boiling water to the millet; return to a boil. Reduce heat to low; simmer, covered, 25 minutes. Transfer the millet to a bowl to cool slightly; tent with foil to prevent from drying out. When cooled, stir in the eggs, salt, and parsley.

2. Bring a large saucepan of salted water to a boil. Meanwhile, cut the broccoli into bite-size pieces. Blanch the broccoli for about 20 seconds, until bright green. Transfer to an ice-water bath to cool. Drain, and set aside.

3. Heat oven to 350°. Melt 1 tablespoon butter in a large saucepan over medium-high heat. Add the onion; cook, stirring occasionally, 5 minutes. Add the cabbage; cook, stirring occasionally, 3 minutes. Add the garlic, ginger, and curry; cook 2 minutes. Pour in 2 cups water, and, using a wooden spoon, scrape up any brown bits on bottom of pan. Add the carrots, potatoes, lentils, and chickpeas, and bring to a boil. Reduce heat to medium low, and simmer, covered, for 20 minutes. Stir in reserved broccoli; season to taste with salt and pepper.

4. Place the stew in a 1¹/₂-quart ovenproof casserole; cover with millet mixture. Dot millet with remaining tablespoon butter; place on a baking sheet. Bake for 30 minutes, until golden brown and crisp. Serve with cucumber raita.

Cucumber Raita   **makes 2 cups**

1³/₄ cups plain yogurt

¹/₂ medium cucumber, peeled and seeded

¹/₂ teaspoon coarse salt

¹/₂ teaspoon ground cumin
Sprig of fresh mint, coarsely chopped, plus more for garnish

Place the yogurt in a medium-size mixing bowl. On the large holes of a box grater, grate the cucumber directly into the bowl. Season the mixture with salt, cumin, and mint, stirring well. Chill the raita slightly. Garnish with chopped mint, and serve.

Coq au Vin

6 large cloves garlic, smashed

4 whole black peppercorns

2 sprigs fresh thyme, plus more for garnish

1 dried bay leaf

7 sprigs fresh flat-leaf parsley, stems and leaves separated

2 tablespoons olive oil

8 ounces pearl onions, peeled

12 ounces white button mushrooms, halved or quartered

2 whole skinless and boneless chicken breasts

1 tablespoon unsalted butter

Salt and freshly ground pepper

3 tablespoons cognac

1 cup dry red wine

3¼ cups Chicken Stock (recipe, page 56), or canned

1 tablespoon tomato paste

1 tablespoon cornstarch

Serve this stew over a grain like rice, barley, or quinoa (pronounced KEEN-wah).   **serves 6**

1. Using a small piece of cheesecloth, make a bouquet garni: Wrap 3 garlic cloves, peppercorns, thyme, bay leaf, and parsley stems; tie in a bundle with kitchen twine. Set aside.

2. In a large, deep skillet or a Dutch oven, heat 1 tablespoon oil over medium-high heat. Add onions and remaining 3 cloves garlic; cook, stirring occasionally, until they begin to brown, about 4 minutes. Add the mushrooms, and cook until golden, about 4 minutes. Transfer to a bowl.

3. Cut the chicken into strips about 2 inches long and ¾ inch wide. Add the butter and remaining 1 tablespoon olive oil to the skillet. Season chicken with salt and pepper; cook in two batches until browned, about 1 minute per side. Return all of the chicken to the skillet. Add the cognac and wine. Use a wooden spoon to scrape up any browned bits on bottom of pan. Add chicken stock; stir in tomato paste. Add bouquet garni. Bring to a boil; reduce heat to a simmer, and cook, covered, 15 minutes. Add the reserved mushrooms, onions, and garlic. Cook 5 minutes more.

4. Using a slotted spoon, transfer the chicken and vegetables to a bowl. Discard bouquet garni. Over high heat, reduce broth by half, about 12 minutes. In a small bowl, dissolve cornstarch in 1 tablespoon cold water. Stir back into broth, and mix until incorporated. Cook 2 minutes. Return chicken, onions, and mushrooms to pot; cook over warm heat until thoroughly warm. Chop parsley leaves, and stir in. Garnish with thyme, and serve.

"My mother made it once a month . . . always on a Saturday night. She served it on our good dishes, and we got to eat in the dining room. She always let me have a few sips of wine with it." —SUSAN SUGARMAN, SENIOR FOOD EDITOR

As comforting as classic French Coq au Vin yet easier to make, this chicken in wine is made with quick-cooking strips of boneless chicken breast in place of a whole cut-up chicken. Sautéed separately at first, the chicken and vegetables then stew together, blending their flavors in a glistening sauce of cognac, red wine, garlic, and fresh herbs.

sides and small suppers

chapter five

Eating, like so many activities, has a public and private face.

The best French fries are the ones you make yourself: hand cut, oven fried, and served hot and salty. Mild malt vinegar is our favorite condiment for drizzling over a heaping pile of fries or for dipping them in one at a time. See recipe, page 100.

When we dine out, we tend to observe the conventions of mealtime. But in private—when no one else is home for dinner, or when at midnight we bravely venture, like a hungry jungle cat, into the kitchen—certain foods crowd into the forefront of our appetites. A baked potato may suddenly loom large in the imagination. As the microwave hums, you rummage in the refrigerator. Minutes later, the skin is split, and you melt butter and four varieties of cheese into the most soul-warming of meals.

This chapter is devoted to the foods that invite us to break the boundaries. You might call them side dishes, but you could just as well call them supper. Foremost among these are potatoes, both white and sweet. We mash, bake, stuff, gratinée, and, of course, fry them; it is hard to describe exactly what is so irresistible about a perfect French fry, but when you make them with the recipe here, you will know the answer. There are also two kinds of risotto and a satisfying spoonbread.

All are simple to prepare and easy to eat ... and eat ... and eat. Some are more texture than flavor, some aggressively spicy; some soft, some crisp, some soft *and* crisp. Each of them better satisfies a certain hunger than anything else. Is there a better definition of comfort food than this?

Potato Torta With Olives

2 large Spanish onions
3 tablespoons olive oil
2 tablespoons fresh rosemary
  Salt and freshly ground pepper
½ cup Gaeta or oil-cured black
  olives, pitted and torn into pieces
6 Yukon gold or Yellow Finn potatoes (about 2¼ pounds), peeled
¼ pound fontina cheese, cubed

A slice of potato torta and a green salad make a delicious supper.   **serves 4 to 6**

1. Cut onions into ½-inch-thick slices. Heat 1 tablespoon oil in a large sauté pan over medium heat. Add onions, and cook, stirring frequently, until golden brown and soft, about 20 minutes.

2. Reduce heat to low, and then add the rosemary and salt and pepper to taste. Cook for about 5 minutes, stirring often. Add the black-olive pieces, and set aside.

3. Heat oven to 400°. Cut 3 of the potatoes into ¼-inch-thick slices. In an 8-inch cast-iron skillet, heat 1 tablespoon oil over medium heat. Arrange potato slices in overlapping circles in the pan. Season with salt and pepper. Spread reserved onion mixture on potatoes. Cook for 10 minutes, not stirring.

4. Dot onions with cheese. Slice remaining potatoes, and arrange a second layer in overlapping circles over onion mixture. Season lightly with salt and pepper, and brush with remaining tablespoon oil. Return skillet to the oven, and bake for 20 to 25 minutes, or until a toothpick goes through easily.

5. Let torta cool 2 to 3 minutes in the pan. Carefully run a small, sharp knife around the edge. Hold skillet with a clean kitchen towel, and invert torta onto a plate. Cut into wedges, and serve.

Lemon and Thyme Potato Gratin

2 tablespoons unsalted butter, plus
  more melted for pan
2 pounds Yukon gold potatoes,
  peeled and very thinly sliced
2 teaspoons chopped fresh thyme
⅛ teaspoon freshly grated nutmeg
  Zest of 1 lemon, finely chopped
  (2 teaspoons)
  Salt and freshly ground pepper
1 cup milk

This is a fragrant variation on classic scalloped potatoes. Baked in milk and laced with lemon zest, the potatoes absorb almost all of the liquid; the last drops thicken into a luscious creamy coating.   **serves 4**

1. Heat oven to 400° with rack in center. Place a baking sheet on rack below to catch any drips from the gratin. Brush a 10-by-5½-inch gratin dish generously with melted butter.

2. Cover bottom of gratin dish with one-third of the potato slices, in an even layer. Sprinkle potatoes with one-third of the thyme, nutmeg, and lemon zest; season to taste with salt and pepper. Dot with butter. Add a second layer of potato slices, and season. Top with a third layer of neatly arranged potato slices. Pour milk over potatoes. Sprinkle with remaining third thyme, nutmeg, and lemon zest, and dot with butter. Season to taste with salt and pepper. Cover with aluminum foil.

3. Bake for 40 minutes. Remove the foil, and continue to bake 10 to 20 minutes more, until the top of the gratin is golden brown and the potatoes are tender when pierced with the tip of a knife. If the top of the gratin is not golden brown but the potatoes are tender, heat the broiler. Place gratin under the broiler for just a few seconds to brown nicely. Serve gratin hot, spooned out into individual servings. Potato gratin will hold well in a low oven (about 200°) if covered with aluminum foil, for 40 minutes to 1 hour.

A skillet layered with thinly sliced
potato rounds, sautéed onions,
and bits of oil-cured black olives
forms our potato torta. First
crisped on the stovetop and then
baked until tender, the "cake"
is turned out of the pan to serve,
so the crustiest golden layer
is on top, with pools of melted
fontina cheese spilling out.

Partners in the oven and on the plate, a baked potato and a whole head of roasted garlic make a heavenly dinner. Our Oven Frites (opposite) have the golden crispiness and soft interior of fine deep-fried potatoes, yet only two tablespoons of oil are needed to prepare them. Cut them into thin sticks called batons, and bake in a single layer.

Baked Potatoes With Roasted Garlic

4 whole heads garlic
Extra-virgin olive oil
4 Idaho baking potatoes
(about 2¼ pounds)
Coarse salt
Freshly ground pepper

Roasted garlic is also good spread on bread and stirred into sauces. Make an extra head or two; it will keep, tightly wrapped, in the refrigerator for up to three days.   **serves 4**

1. Using a sharp knife, score each garlic head an inch from the top. Peel away the top inch of skin.

2. Heat oven to 425°. Rub heads of garlic lightly with olive oil, and wrap them loosely in aluminum foil. Bake garlic and potatoes until garlic is very soft and potatoes are tender, about 1 hour. Serve each potato with a head of garlic; let guests squeeze the roasted garlic from the skin and mix it into the baked potato along with coarse salt, pepper, and olive oil as desired.

Oven Frites

4 medium baking potatoes
2 tablespoons olive oil
1½ teaspoons salt
¼ teaspoon freshly ground pepper
Malt vinegar (optional)

Serve these baked French fries with a bowl of malt vinegar. They are also delicious dipped in spicy mustard, mayonnaise, and, of course, ketchup.   **serves 4**

1. Heat oven to 400°. Place a heavy baking sheet in the oven. Scrub and rinse the potatoes well, and then cut them lengthwise into ½-inch-wide batons. Place the potato batons in a medium bowl, and toss them with the olive oil, salt, and pepper.

2. When baking sheet is hot, about 15 minutes, remove from the oven. Place prepared potatoes on the baking sheet in a single layer. Return to oven, and bake until potatoes are golden on the bottom, about 30 minutes. Turn potatoes over, and continue cooking until golden all over, about 15 minutes more. Serve immediately.

"Crispy, greasy, salty: my three favorite flavors."

—MELISSA MORGAN, MANAGING EDITOR

Salt and Vinegar Potato Chips

4 medium Yukon gold or
red potatoes, scrubbed
(about 2½ pounds)
2 tablespoons olive oil
1 teaspoon salt
½ teaspoon freshly ground pepper
Malt vinegar for drizzling

Avoid stirring or turning the potatoes as they bake on each side. Moving them around will cause them to stick, tearing the crispy surface from the chip.   **serves 4**

1. Heat oven to 425°. Place two baking sheets in the oven, and let heat for about 10 minutes.

2. Slice the potatoes into ¼-inch-thick rounds. Toss the potatoes with the olive oil, salt, and pepper.

3. Remove the baking sheets from the oven, and arrange potato slices on sheets in a single layer. Bake until the potatoes are golden on the bottom side, about 30 minutes. Turn potatoes over, and bake until they are golden brown all over, about 15 minutes more. Remove from oven, drizzle with vinegar, and serve immediately.

Salted, baked, and then drizzled with malt vinegar, oven-crisped potato chips are piled in a parchment-lined antique colander. Cut Yukon gold or red potatoes into thick rounds, and then toss them with olive oil, salt, and pepper before they are oven-fried. The chips are best eaten right after they are made.

Carrot and Parsnip Purée

2 tablespoons unsalted butter
1 teaspoon extra-virgin olive oil
4 medium parsnips, peeled and cut into ¹/₂-inch dice
1 bunch carrots, peeled and cut into ¹/₄-inch dice
¹/₂ small onion, coarsely chopped
1 clove garlic, coarsely chopped
¹/₂ cup Chicken Stock (page 56), or canned
  Salt and freshly ground pepper
6 chives, for garnish

Celery root, rutabagas, and turnips can be substituted for the parsnips in this recipe. Because carrots are firmer and take longer to cook than parsnips, they are cut slightly smaller for even cooking.   **serves 4**

1. Blend butter and olive oil in a medium saucepan over medium heat. Add the remaining ingredients, except the chives. Salt and pepper to taste. Add ¹/₂ cup water; cook, covered, until vegetables are tender when pierced with the tip of a knife, about 30 minutes.

2. Transfer vegetables to a food processor or blender, and purée. Spoon into a serving dish, garnish with chives, and serve immediately.

Twice-Baked Squash

6 butternut squash (about 9 pounds total)
1¹/₂ teaspoons salt, plus more to taste
¹/₂ teaspoon freshly ground pepper, plus more to taste
9 tablespoons sour cream
2 teaspoons paprika
6 chives, cut into ¹/₈-inch pieces
3 tablespoons fresh bread crumbs, lightly toasted

A variation on another twice-baked favorite, the potato, two squash halves make a delicious vegetarian dinner. Serve with mâche or a mixed green salad.   **serves 6**

1. Heat oven to 450° with the rack in center. Halve the squash lengthwise, and remove the seeds and fibers. Sprinkle squash halves with ¹/₂ teaspoon salt and ¹/₄ teaspoon pepper. Fill a roasting pan with ¹/₄ inch water. Place squash in pan. Cover with aluminum foil, and bake until squash is tender when pierced with the tip of a knife, 35 to 45 minutes. Remove from oven, transfer squash to a cool surface, and let cool enough to handle. Reduce oven temperature to 425°.

2. Use a spoon to scoop the baked flesh out of each half, leaving a ¹/₄-inch border around six of the halves so they will keep their shape. To the bowl, add the sour cream, paprika, chives, and remaining teaspoon salt and ¹/₄ teaspoon pepper. Mix with a handheld electric mixer or potato masher until smooth and well combined. Taste, and adjust seasoning with salt and pepper. Fill the six squash halves with the mixture (discard the remaining six empty halves). Sprinkle the toasted bread crumbs on top. Bake until golden brown and warm throughout, 20 to 30 minutes. Serve.

Warm and creamy Carrot and Parsnip Purée is little more than these sweet-natured root vegetables blended with onion, garlic, butter, and chicken stock. Another smooth vegetable mash fills the shells of our Twice-Baked Squash (below). Scoop out the soft flesh after the first baking, mix with sour cream and paprika, top with bread crumbs, and then return to the oven. Puffed and golden, serve the squash halves with a garnish of crispy mâche or other small salad green.

"A vegetable equivalent of honey and cream." —FRANCES BOSWELL, DEPUTY FOOD EDITOR

Part pudding, part soufflé, every airy bite of spoon bread is corn—sweet and savory at the same time. The cornmeal base is lightened with whipped egg whites, laden with leeks and cut-from-the-cob kernels, and seasoned with cayenne. Easier than sweet-potato pie and just as pretty, small oven-baked sweet potatoes (opposite) are split and crowned with sour cream and brown sugar.

Perfect Mashed Potatoes

2 pounds russet, Yukon gold, or long white potatoes

1 tablespoon salt, plus more to taste

1 cup milk or cream

4 tablespoons unsalted butter, cut into pieces

¼ teaspoon freshly ground pepper

¼ teaspoon freshly grated nutmeg

If you prefer stiffer mashed potatoes, use only three-quarters cup milk or cream; to make even richer potatoes, include an additional two tablespoons of butter.   **serves 4 to 6**

1. Peel and cut potatoes into 1½-inch-thick slices. Place in a medium saucepan. Cover with cold water and add the salt; bring to a simmer. If using a potato ricer, fill another saucepan or the bottom of a double boiler with water, and place over low heat. Simmer potatoes until a knife easily slips in and out of them, 20 to 25 minutes. Drain potatoes in a colander.

2. Place milk in a small saucepan set over medium-high heat. (If using an electric mixer fit with the paddle attachment, proceed to step 4.) If using a potato ricer, place a heat-proof bowl or the top of a double boiler over the pan of simmering water. Press hot, drained potatoes through ricer into bowl.

3. Stir potatoes with a wooden spoon until smooth, about 1 minute. Using a whisk, incorporate the butter. Drizzle in the hot milk, whisking continuously. Add pepper, nutmeg, and salt to taste; whisk to combine. Serve immediately.

4. For the electric-mixer method, transfer hot, drained potatoes to bowl of electric mixer fitted with the paddle attachment. Mix on medium-low speed, until most lumps have disappeared, about 1 minute. Add butter; mix until blended. On low speed, add the hot milk in a slow stream, then add pepper, nutmeg, and salt to taste. Mix to combine.

mashed-potato mix-ins

SAFFRON MASHED POTATOES While heating the milk for mashed potatoes, add a generous pinch of saffron. Allow to steep in milk 5 minutes. Add milk to potatoes, and mash.

GARLIC MASHED POTATOES Add 3 smashed garlic cloves to milk. Cover, and simmer until garlic is mild and soft, about 20 minutes. Add milk and garlic directly to potatoes, and mash.

ROASTED-GARLIC MASHED POTATOES Wrap a small head of garlic in aluminum foil, and place in the oven at 400° for 45 minutes. When cool enough to handle, peel roasted garlic, and add to potatoes, to taste, while mashing.

HERBED MASHED POTATOES Add fresh chopped herbs such as parsley, dill, chives, or basil to mashed potatoes. Or to make bright-green potatoes, substitute any herb-infused olive oil for the butter. To make it, purée herbs and olive oil in the bowl of a food processor until herbs are finely minced and olive oil is bright green.

MASHED POTATOES AND ROOT VEGETABLES Substitute 6 ounces cooked carrots, sweet potatoes, celery root, or turnips for 6 ounces potatoes.

Match mashed potatoes to your meal—or your mood: Make them lumpy or creamy; with extra butter, a drizzle of olive oil, or a head of roasted garlic. Make them ivory white or flecked with black pepper; saffron-gold, herb-green, or carrot-orange. Steaming and soft, they're comforting in every color.

Baked Sweet Potatoes
With Sour Cream and Brown Sugar

4   medium sweet potatoes (about
     2½ pounds)
1   tablespoon vegetable oil
     Salt and freshly ground pepper
½   cup sour cream
4   teaspoons dark-brown sugar

Rubbing a little vegetable oil on the potato before baking adds a nice sheen and flavor to the skin.   **serves 4**

1. Heat oven to 400°. Line a baking sheet with parchment paper or aluminum foil, and set aside. Rub the potatoes with vegetable oil, and place on the prepared baking sheet. Bake in the oven until the potatoes can be easily pierced with a knife, 40 to 45 minutes.

2. Slit the potatoes open lengthwise, and sprinkle with salt and pepper. Top with a generous dollop of the sour cream, sprinkle with the dark-brown sugar, and serve immediately.

Spoon Bread With Leeks and Corn

    Butter, for greasing
3   large eggs, separated
2½   cups milk
½   teaspoon cayenne pepper
1   teaspoon salt
1   cup yellow cornmeal, preferably
     stone-ground
2   teaspoons baking powder
1   cup fresh corn (cut from 2 or 3
     yellow or white ears)
2   leeks, halved lengthwise, thinly
     sliced and well washed

Any shape of dish can be used, but spoon bread will bake best in one that is slightly wider than it is high. If the dish is narrow and deep, the baking time will be slightly longer. Baking time should be adjusted to dish size.   **serves 8**

1. Heat oven to 400°. Butter a 6-cup baking dish. Lightly beat egg yolks; set aside.

2. In a saucepan over medium heat, bring 2 cups of the milk, the cayenne, and salt to a boil. Sprinkle cornmeal into liquid, stirring constantly, and cook until thick and smooth, about 3 minutes. Stir in remaining ½ cup milk, baking powder, and egg yolks.

3. In a mixing bowl, beat egg whites until stiff. Stir 1 large spoonful of whites into cornmeal mixture to lighten, then gently fold in remaining whites.

4. Pour half of the batter into prepared dish. Sprinkle on corn and leeks. Cover with remaining batter. Bake until set and golden brown, 35 to 40 minutes. Serve immediately.

"My mother swears that baked sweet potatoes taste better cold than hot. They're sweeter, but best of all, they're portable. She always embarrassed me by sneaking one into my lunchbox. Now I eat them late at night, standing in front of the fridge, skin and all." —JENNIFER HERMAN, ASSISTANT FOOD EDITOR

Parsnip Pierogies With Pickled Red Cabbage Slaw and Sautéed Apples

The pierogies can be assembled ahead of time and refrigerated on a lightly floured baking sheet, with waxed paper between the layers to keep them from sticking together.　**makes 2 dozen**

PICKLED RED CABBAGE SLAW

- ¼ cup red-wine vinegar
- 1½ tablespoons sugar
- 1 teaspoon caraway seeds, crushed
- ¼ small red cabbage, finely shredded
  Salt and freshly ground pepper

PIEROGI DOUGH

- 1 large egg
- ½ cup milk
- 1½ tablespoons sour cream
- 2¼ cups all-purpose flour, or more as needed

PIEROGI FILLING

- 1½ pounds parsnips, peeled
- 2 shallots, peeled
- 1 teaspoon unsalted butter
  Freshly grated nutmeg
  Salt and freshly ground pepper
- 2 teaspoons freshly grated or prepared horseradish
- 4 ounces farmer cheese or goat cheese

SAUTÉED APPLES

- 2 teaspoons unsalted butter
- 2 apples, peeled if desired, cored, and thinly sliced
- 1 tablespoon sugar

1. To make red-cabbage slaw, whisk together vinegar, sugar, and caraway seeds in a medium bowl. Toss in cabbage. Season with salt and pepper. Let marinate for at least 1 hour, or overnight.

2. To make pierogi dough, whisk together egg, milk, sour cream, and ½ cup water. Stir in flour a little at a time until dough comes together. Turn out onto a lightly floured board, and knead until smooth and elastic, up to 10 minutes. Incorporate more flour if dough is too sticky. Cover dough with plastic wrap, and allow to rest for 1 hour.

3. To make filling, place parsnips in a medium saucepan, and cover with cold, salted water. Bring to a boil, and simmer until tender, 20 to 25 minutes. Drain and put through a food mill to purée.

4. In a small sauté pan, cook shallots in butter until soft, stirring occasionally, 1 to 2 minutes. Stir shallots into purée, and add nutmeg, salt, and pepper to taste. Remove from heat, and let cool slightly, then mix in horseradish and cheese.

5. On a lightly floured board, roll out dough to ⅛ inch. Cut out circles using a 3¾-inch-round cutter. Set circles aside on a floured tray. Place a round tablespoon of filling on each circle. Lightly wet edges, fold over, and seal by pinching.

6. To make sautéed apples, heat a medium sauté pan over medium-high heat. Melt butter, add apple slices, and toss to coat. Add sugar and toss again to coat evenly. Cook until brown, about 5 minutes.

7. When ready to serve, bring a pot of salted water to a boil. Add pierogies, and cook for 5 minutes after they float to the surface; drain. Pierogies can be eaten right away or browned in a small amount of butter. Serve with red-cabbage slaw and sautéed apples.

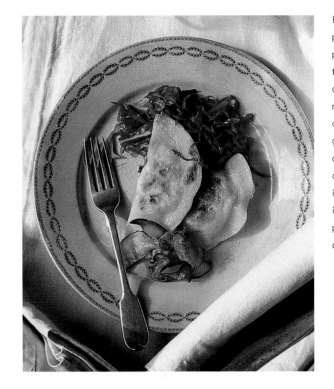

Butter-glazed apples, quick-pickled red cabbage, and stuffed pierogies are all delicious by themselves, but together this trio of traditional Polish dishes makes a satisfying supper—one of Martha's favorites. Piero-gies are filled dumplings—circles of sour-cream dough folded over a meat or vegetable stuffing, briefly boiled and browned in butter. Ours are filled with puréed parsnip, mild farmer cheese, and fresh horseradish.

Parmesan Risotto

6 cups Chicken Stock
   (page 56), or canned

1½ tablespoons unsalted butter

1½ tablespoons olive oil

6 cloves garlic, minced

2 medium shallots, minced

2 cups Arborio rice (or other
   short-grain white rice)

1 cup dry white wine
   Zest of 1 lemon (2 teaspoons),
   plus more for garnish (optional)

¾ cup freshly grated Parmesan
   cheese (about 2 ounces), plus
   more for garnish

1½ teaspoons salt

¼ teaspoon freshly ground pepper

A generous amount of Parmesan, stirred into the rice just before serving, gives this risotto its exceptionally creamy texture. Always buy whole chunks of Parmesan and grate it just before using for the best flavor.   **serves 4 to 6**

1. Heat the chicken stock in a medium saucepan, and keep hot throughout risotto preparation.

2. Heat butter and oil in a large, heavy saucepan over medium heat. Add garlic and shallots, and sauté, stirring occasionally, until softened and translucent, 3 to 4 minutes. Do not brown. Add rice, and stir to coat. Cook rice, stirring frequently, until well coated and grains start to appear translucent, about 2 minutes. Add wine, and stir constantly until it has evaporated, about 2 minutes.

3. Add 1 cup of the hot stock, and cook, stirring constantly, until almost all of the liquid has evaporated. Then add ½ cup hot stock at a time, stirring constantly until each addition is absorbed (set aside about ½ cup stock to adjust consistency when serving). Cook the mixture until the rice is tender but still firm in the center; the time varies, but generally it is 20 to 25 minutes.

4. Remove pan from heat, and stir in 2 teaspoons lemon zest, ¾ cup Parmesan cheese, salt, and pepper. Add some of the remaining hot stock a little at a time to reach desired consistency. Serve immediately, garnished with additional lemon zest, if desired, and Parmesan cheese.

Baked Sage and Saffron Risotto

2 tablespoons olive oil

3 shallots, minced

1 cup Arborio rice

⅛ teaspoon saffron threads

½ cup dry white wine

2 cups Chicken Stock
   (page 56), or canned

6 fresh sage leaves, coarsely
   chopped (about 1 tablespoon),
   plus more for garnish

1 teaspoon salt

⅛ teaspoon freshly ground pepper

1 tablespoon unsalted butter, cut
   into small pieces

When risotto is baked rather than cooked on the stove, it does not require constant stirring.   **serves 4**

1. Heat oven to 450°. In a medium ovenproof saucepan, heat oil over medium heat. Add the shallots; cook, stirring until shallots are translucent, 2 to 3 minutes. Add rice, and stir until grains are shiny and well coated with oil, about 2 minutes more. Add saffron and wine, and continue cooking and stirring until liquid is absorbed, 3 to 5 minutes.

2. Add stock, sage, salt, and pepper. Cover saucepan; transfer to oven. Bake until all of the stock is absorbed and rice is tender, about 25 minutes.

3. Remove the cover from saucepan. Dot the top of the rice with butter, arrange sage over the rice, and bake until the butter is melted, about 5 minutes more. Serve immediately.

Short plump grains of Arborio rice give authentic risotto a delightfully creamy texture. Our simple baked risotto, gilded with saffron and fragrant with fresh sage, is a glowing sight served in a deep ceramic baking dish. Parmesan Risotto (opposite inset) is made the traditional way—slowly cooked and stirred on the stove as the rice swells with liquid, and then seasoned just before serving.

Classic Caesar Salad

FOR THE CROUTONS:

- 2 tablespoons unsalted butter, melted
- 2 tablespoons extra-virgin olive oil
- 1 eight- to ten-ounce loaf rustic Italian bread, crusts removed, cut into ¾-inch cubes
- 2 teaspoons salt
- ¼ teaspoon ground cayenne pepper
- ½ teaspoon freshly ground black pepper

FOR THE SALAD:

- 2 cloves garlic
- 4 anchovy fillets
- 1 teaspoon salt
- 1 teaspoon freshly ground black pepper
- 1 tablespoon freshly squeezed lemon juice
- 1 teaspoon Worcestershire sauce
- ½ teaspoon Dijon mustard
- 1 large egg yolk
- ⅓ cup extra-virgin olive oil
- 2 ten-ounce heads romaine lettuce, outer leaves discarded, inner leaves washed and dried
- 1 cup freshly grated Parmesan or Romano cheese, or 2½ ounces shaved with a vegetable peeler

If you prefer not to use the raw yolk in this recipe, substitute one tablespoon of store-bought mayonnaise. Extra Parmesan can be grated over the top of the salad as a garnish. The croutons are best made no more than half an hour before assembling the salad.   **serves 4 to 6**

1. Heat oven to 450°. Combine the butter and olive oil in a large bowl. Add the cubes of bread, and toss until coated. Sprinkle the salt, cayenne pepper, and black pepper; toss until evenly coated. Spread the bread in a single layer on an 11-by-17-inch baking sheet. Bake until the croutons are golden, about 10 minutes. Set aside until needed.

2. Place the garlic, anchovy fillets, and salt in a large wooden salad bowl. Using two dinner forks, mash the garlic and anchovies into a paste.

3. Using one fork, whisk in pepper, lemon juice, Worcestershire, Dijon mustard, and egg yolk.

4. Using the fork, whisk in the olive oil. To make a version of this dressing that you can store, simply mince the garlic and anchovies, and place with the remaining ingredients in a jar. Screw the lid on the jar tightly, and shake to combine. Shake the jar before each use. Store, refrigerated, up to 4 days.

5. Chop the romaine leaves into 1- to 1½-inch pieces. Add the croutons, romaine, and cheese to the bowl, and toss well. Serve immediately.

Crisp, pale-green romaine leaves and toasted pepper-and-butter croutons are tossed with the traditional dressing of anchovy, egg yolk, garlic, olive oil, lemon juice, and Worcestershire in this Classic Caesar Salad. A generous dusting of grated Parmesan cheese floats on the surface.

sweet endings

chapter six

Everybody, no matter what they say, has a sweet tooth.

A dark fudgy brownie and a cold glass of milk make life worth living. Baked in crinkled cupcake papers, they can be packed into a lunchbox or a briefcase. Brownie-making is easy; only hand-mixing is required—but the best-quality chocolate, unsalted butter, and pure vanilla extract are absolutely essential. See recipe, page 136.

Fortunately, for most of us it is one tooth we never lose. Remember how marvelous it was to come home to home-made cookies waiting on the kitchen table? Bring a plate of our chewy oatmeal-raisin cookies to the office, and the smiles will show that sweet treats still have enormous power to please.

Here is a selection of sweets to distract even the busiest workaholic. You'll find brownies for packing into picnic baskets, puddings to end a dinner party, and cakes to crown with a circle of birthday candles.

Sweet flavor alone doesn't make the desserts in this chapter comforting. Their texture, too, is easy to love. Consider the gentle creaminess of silky vanilla custard or luscious caramel pots

de crème; the melting softness of maple-syrup-soaked baked apples with ricotta cream; the familiar crumble and snap of homemade peanut-butter cookies. There's the warmth of chocolate bread pudding, and of cobbler fresh from the oven, bubbling with fresh blackberries and blueberries; and the chill of a double-decker malted milk shake. And sometimes the sheer fun of it is enough: a classic soda-fountain treat—three kinds of ice cream, three rich toppings, a banana, plus, of course, mounds of whipped cream and cherries on top.

Vanilla Custard

1¼ cups heavy cream

1¼ cups milk

1 vanilla bean, split, or 2 teaspoons pure vanilla extract

6 large egg yolks

½ cup sugar

Good-quality vanilla extract can be used in custards, but a fresh vanilla bean will add the best flavor.　**serves 4**

1. Heat oven to 300° with an oven rack one-third of the way up from the bottom. Choose a small roasting pan large enough to hold four 6-ounce custard cups, and fill it with enough water to go halfway up the sides of cups. Place the pan, without the cups, in the oven. Meanwhile, combine the cream, milk, and the vanilla bean, if using, in a medium saucepan, and bring to boil. Remove from heat. Allow to steep, covered, for 10 minutes. Scrape the vanilla seeds from the pod into the hot cream mixture, and discard the pod. Stir well to disperse the seeds, and set aside.

2. Whisk together the egg yolks and sugar in a medium bowl until light and fluffy. Slowly whisk in the hot-milk mixture until completely combined. (Whisk in vanilla extract, if using.) Pour mixture into the custard cups. Place them in the pan of hot water. Bake until the custard has set and is no longer liquid when lightly touched in the center, 30 to 40 minutes. Remove pan from the oven, remove custard cups from the water, and place on a wire rack to cool. Serve at room temperature or chilled.

Coffee Custard

Unsalted butter, melted, for custard cups

1 cup heavy cream

½ cup milk

2 tablespoons instant espresso powder

3 large egg yolks

1 large whole egg

¼ cup sugar

1 teaspoon pure vanilla extract

Pinch of salt

¼ cup dark chocolate shavings (about 1 ounce)

Espresso paired with chocolate produces a soothing mocha custard—delicious warm or chilled.　**serves 4**

1. Place a roasting pan three-quarters full of hot water in a 300° oven. Brush four 6-ounce custard cups with melted butter. Set aside. Combine the cream, milk, and espresso in a small saucepan over medium heat, and bring almost to a simmer. Remove from heat, and set aside.

2. Whisk together egg yolks, whole egg, sugar, vanilla, and a pinch of salt in a medium bowl. Add a little of the hot milk mixture to the egg mixture, and whisk well. Add the remaining milk mixture, and whisk again to combine well. Strain mixture through a sieve. Pour into the custard cups and place in water bath in the oven, making sure that the water comes three-quarters of the way up sides of cups. Bake until the custard is set, about 35 minutes.

3. Remove from the oven and water bath. Cool for about 20 minutes. Loosen custards with a knife. Invert onto serving dishes; top with chocolate. Alternatively, refrigerate and turn out when needed.

Laced with espresso and topped with dark chocolate shavings, an unmolded coffee custard—shimmering and dark—brings a mature taste to the innocent pleasure of custard.

A fluted cup of Vanilla Custard is a pure and simple path to comfort: Savor the golden cream, flecked with tiny, fragrant seeds from a vanilla bean, spoonful by spoonful. Although a garnish is not necessary, ripe raspberries provide a colorful and tart accent.

Spiked with a cinnamon stick and still warm from the oven, a rosy baked apple (right) is glazed with maple syrup and its own sweet apple juices. A scoop of lightly spiced and puréed ricotta cheese makes a creamy and cool frosting for each bite of tender fruit. Soft, sweet, and hot contrasts delightfully with soft, sweet, and cold when you top off a bowl of chilled rice pudding (below) with just-caramelized, buttery banana slices.

Baked Apples With Spiced Ricotta and Maple Syrup

4 medium Rome apples (8 ounces each), cored to within 1/2 inch of base

3 tablespoons unsalted butter

6 tablespoons pure maple syrup

1 teaspoon freshly grated ginger

4 three-inch-long cinnamon sticks

3/4 cup ricotta cheese

2 tablespoons plus 1 teaspoon confectioners' sugar

1/8 teaspoon ground cinnamon

3 tablespoons heavy cream

The best baking apples have full flavor, firm flesh, and moderate juiciness. Aside from Rome apples, other good varieties include Cortland, Baldwin, Empire, and Northern Spy. Baking times will vary with size and variety; check apples in the oven frequently for softness by squeezing or piercing with a sharp knife.   serves 4

1. Heat oven to 450°. Peel about 1 inch of skin from tops of apples; cut a sliver off the bottom so apples will stand. Place them in a 9-inch glass pie plate. Cut 1 tablespoon of butter into 4 pieces; fill each apple core with a piece of butter, 1 tablespoon maple syrup, 1/8 teaspoon ginger, and 1 cinnamon stick. Place remaining 2 tablespoons butter and 2 tablespoons syrup in bottom of pie plate.

2. Bake the apples, basting them several times with the juices at the bottom of the pie plate, until they are golden and tender, about 35 minutes (the skin may split). Transfer apples to a serving dish; let juices stand to thicken, about 15 minutes.

3. Purée the ricotta, confectioners' sugar, remaining ginger, ground cinnamon, and cream in the bowl of a food processor. Serve 2 heaping tablespoons of ricotta cream with each apple. Drizzle with warm syrup from the bottom of the pie plate.

Creamy Rice Pudding With Caramelized Bananas

3 cups milk

1 cup heavy cream

1 vanilla bean, split

3/4 cup plus 6 tablespoons sugar
Pinch of salt

1 cinnamon stick
Pinch of freshly grated nutmeg

1/2 cup long-grain white rice

2 large egg yolks

3 tablespoons unsalted butter

3 ripe but firm medium bananas

1 teaspoon freshly squeezed lemon juice

Make the rice pudding in the morning or a day ahead of time if serving with the warm bananas. Or enjoy it warm or at room temperature with a splash of cold heavy cream.   serves 6

1. In a medium saucepan, combine 1 cup of milk, the cream, vanilla bean, 6 tablespoons sugar, a pinch of salt, the cinnamon, and the nutmeg. Bring to a boil, then remove from heat, and let stand, covered, for 30 minutes.

2. Bring a small saucepan of water to a boil, add rice, and blanch for 1 to 2 minutes. Drain, and set aside. Remove vanilla bean and cinnamon stick from milk mixture. Scrape seeds from bean, and stir them back into the mixture; discard bean and cinnamon. Stir in blanched rice, and cook, covered, over low heat, stirring occasionally, until liquid is mostly absorbed, about 1 hour.

3. In a small bowl, whisk together egg yolks and remaining 2 cups milk. Add to rice mixture, stirring well. Cook over medium heat, stirring constantly, until thickened, 10 to 15 minutes. Do not allow to boil. Add 1 tablespoon butter, and stir until melted. Remove pudding from heat, transfer to a bowl, and let cool slightly. Chill in refrigerator, covered, 2 1/2 to 3 hours or until cold. Pudding will keep, refrigerated, for up to 3 days.

4. When ready to serve, cut bananas into 1/2-inch-thick diagonal slices. Melt remaining 2 tablespoons butter over medium heat in a heavy skillet. Stir in remaining 3/4 cup sugar and lemon juice, and cook, carefully swirling pan until a golden caramel forms. Add bananas, and cook, stirring occasionally, just until they soften and are coated with caramel, 2 to 3 minutes. Transfer pudding to individual dishes, top with hot bananas, and serve immediately.

A cascade of whipped crème fraîche spills over a serving of Chocolate Bread Pudding, still warm from the oven. Soaking brioche slices in a rich chocolatey custard and slow-baking them transforms the bread into a meltingly tender dark dessert.

Small clouds of whipped cream float on the flawless surface of chilled Caramel Pots de Crème. The most delicately textured of all custards, pots de crème are traditionally baked in tiny porcelain pots with lids. These gain their color and deep flavor from a base of golden-brown caramelized sugar stirred into vanilla-infused cream.

Banana Bread Pudding

2 tablespoons unsalted butter, plus more for ramekins

1¼ cups heavy cream

3 large eggs

¾ cup packed dark-brown sugar

½ teaspoon salt

2 teaspoons pure vanilla extract

2 tablespoons dark rum

3 small bananas (about 1 pound), sliced into ¼-inch-thick rounds

8 ounces peasant bread (about half a loaf), crust removed, torn into 32 small pieces

Layer the bread, banana pieces, and custard in batches, so every bit of pudding is thoroughly moist.   **serves 4**

1. Heat oven to 325°. Place a baking pan filled with ½ inch of water in the center of the oven. Butter four 6-ounce ramekins; set aside. Whisk together cream, eggs, ½ cup sugar, salt, vanilla, and rum; set aside.

2. Cut butter into 8 pieces. Place 1 piece of butter and ½ teaspoon sugar in each ramekin. Place an eighth of the banana slices in an even layer over butter and sugar. Cover banana slices with 4 pieces of bread; sprinkle each with ½ teaspoon sugar. Pour about half the cream mixture among ramekins to soak bread. Divide remaining banana slices among ramekins; sprinkle each with ½ teaspoon sugar. Top with the remaining bread. Pour remaining cream mixture over. Press to soak bread. Place 1 piece of butter in each; sprinkle with remaining sugar.

3. Cover each ramekin loosely with aluminum foil, and bake in the hot-water bath for 30 minutes. Uncover. Bake 30 minutes more. Let ramekins cool on a wire rack for about 30 minutes before serving.

Chocolate Bread Pudding

2 cups heavy cream

2 cups milk

1 vanilla bean, split

3 cinnamon sticks (optional)

1 loaf brioche or good-quality white bread (about 1 pound)

12 ounces bittersweet chocolate, roughly chopped, plus ½ ounce or ¼ cup shavings for garnish

8 large egg yolks

¾ cup sugar

1 eight-ounce container crème fraîche

Use a day-old loaf of brioche or good-quality white bread for this pudding, but don't remove the crusts. If made ahead and refrigerated, you can reheat the whole pudding, covered with foil.   **serves 8 to 10**

1. Heat the oven to 325°. Place the cream, milk, vanilla seeds and pod, and cinnamon sticks, if using, in a medium saucepan, and bring to a boil. Remove from heat, cover with plastic, and let sit for 30 minutes to infuse flavors.

2. Cut the brioche into ¼-inch-thick slices. Cut each slice into quarters, setting aside the rounded top pieces. Fill a 9-by-12 inch gratin dish (you may also use a 9-by-13-inch glass baking dish) with the pieces of bread.

3. Return milk mixture to a boil, remove from heat, and discard vanilla pod and cinnamon sticks. Add chocolate, and whisk until smooth. Combine egg yolks and sugar in a large bowl. Whisk to combine. Very slowly pour chocolate mixture into egg-yolk mixture, whisking constantly, until fully combined.

4. Slowly pour half of the chocolate mixture over bread, making sure that all bread is thoroughly soaked. Arrange the reserved bread tops on top in a decorative pattern, and press firmly so bottom layer of bread absorbs chocolate mixture. Spoon remaining chocolate mixture over bread until completely covered and all cracks are filled. Place a piece of plastic wrap over dish, and press down to soak bread thoroughly. Remove plastic, wipe edges of the dish with a damp towel, and allow to sit for 30 minutes. Place dish in a larger pan, and fill with hot water halfway up the sides of the gratin dish. Bake until set, about 35 minutes. Cool on a rack for 15 minutes before serving. Whisk crème fraîche until soft peaks form. Serve pudding warm garnished with crème fraîche and chocolate shavings.

Caramel Pots de Crème

3/4 cup sugar

1 1/2 cups heavy cream

1 cup milk

1 vanilla bean, split

5 large egg yolks

1/4 teaspoon salt

The name of this delicate dessert comes from the small lidded porcelain pots in which the desserts are traditionally baked. Be careful not to overcook them; the custard should wiggle gently when shaken.   **makes 6**

1. Heat oven to 300°. Place six 4-ounce ovenproof ramekins or pots de crème in a 13-by-9-by-2-inch roasting pan; set aside.

2. Place 1/2 cup sugar in a medium saucepan set over medium heat. Cook, without stirring, until sugar has caramelized and is golden brown, about 3 minutes. Swirl pan, dissolving unmelted sugar; reduce heat to low.

3. Slowly and carefully whisk in 1 cup cream and the milk. Scrape the vanilla seeds into the pan, and add the pod. Increase heat to medium high, and bring to a boil; remove the pan from heat.

4. In a medium bowl, whisk together the remaining 1/4 cup sugar, egg yolks, and salt; continue whisking until pale yellow in color. Slowly add the hot cream mixture to the egg mixture, whisking constantly. Pour this new mixture through a fine sieve set over a large liquid measuring cup; discard vanilla pod.

5. Using a tablespoon or a small ladle, skim the surface to remove any visible air bubbles. Pour approximately 1/2 cup liquid into each ramekin. Fill roasting pan with hot water to within 1 inch of ramekin tops. Cover roasting pan with foil, and poke small holes in two opposite corners for vents.

6. Carefully place pan on center oven rack; bake until just set, about 35 minutes. Remove foil; transfer ramekins to a wire rack to cool completely. Cover with plastic wrap, and refrigerate.

7. When ready to serve, place the remaining 1/2 cup cream in a chilled mixing bowl. Using an electric mixer, whip cream until soft peaks form. Add a dollop of whipped cream to each serving.

Old-Fashioned Tapioca With Sautéed Nectarines

3 tablespoons quick-cooking tapioca

1/4 cup sugar

1/4 cup honey

1/4 teaspoon salt

2 large eggs

2 cups milk

2 large nectarines (about 10 ounces total), each sliced into 10 wedges

1/4 teaspoon ground ginger

4 sprigs fresh mint (optional)

This pudding is delicious with almost any fruit. Substitute fresh peach or apricot wedges for the nectarines, or serve with a warm fruit compote or Stewed Fruit (recipe, page 15).   **serves 4**

1. Combine the tapioca, sugar, 2 tablespoons honey, salt, eggs, and milk in a medium saucepan, and whisk to combine. Let the mixture stand, without stirring, for about 5 minutes. Cook over medium heat, stirring, until the mixture comes to a full boil.

2. Transfer the mixture to a medium bowl set over a large bowl of ice water. Let stand to cool, stirring occasionally, 12 to 15 minutes. When cool, pudding can be refrigerated for up to 1 day before serving.

3. Meanwhile, heat the remaining 2 tablespoons honey in a medium skillet over medium heat. Add the nectarine wedges, and sprinkle them with ground ginger. Cook until the fruit is just tender, 2 to 3 minutes. Divide the tapioca among 4 dishes, and spoon the nectarine mixture over the tops. Garnish each dish of tapioca with a sprig of mint, if desired, and serve.

This regal, amber Classic Flan bathed in caramel glistens on an ivory plate. Coat the baking ramekins with caramel before adding the custard, and you will have a dark sweet sauce when the flans are unmolded. An elegant and versatile dessert, flans can be baked in molds of many sizes, and can be made richer with cream and egg yolks or lighter with milk and whole eggs.

Classic Flan

4 cups milk

½ vanilla bean or 1 teaspoon
pure vanilla extract

1 cinnamon stick or ⅛ teaspoon
ground cinnamon

¾ cup plus 2 tablespoons sugar

4 large eggs

2 tablespoons coffee liqueur
(optional)

Our flan mixture is flavored with vanilla bean, coffee liqueur, and cinnamon, but you can vary the flavor of the custard with other extracts, liqueurs, or citrus zest.　　**serves 6**

1. In a large saucepan, bring the milk, vanilla, cinnamon, and 2 tablespoons sugar to a boil. (If using vanilla bean, split pod lengthwise, and scrape the beans into the milk.) Reduce the heat to a high simmer, and let milk reduce to 2 cups, stirring frequently, 30 to 35 minutes.

2. Place six 6-ounce custard cups in a 2-inch-deep baking pan. Heat oven to 350°.

3. Place ¼ cup water and remaining ¾ cup sugar in a heavy saucepan. Cover, and bring to a boil over high heat until sugar dissolves. Uncover; reduce heat to medium high. Boil until syrup darkens to a light amber color, about 10 minutes. Do not stir. Immediately pour into custard cups, swirling caramel up the sides.

4. Whisk together eggs in a large bowl. Slowly beat in hot reduced milk mixture. Strain the mixture, then pour it into the custard cups.

5. Fill baking pan with ½ inch of warm water, and cover with a tent of aluminum foil. Bake until custards are just set, 30 to 40 minutes. Remove pan from oven, and remove custards from pan. Serve when cooled, or cover flans with plastic wrap, and refrigerate until ready to unmold.

6. To unmold, run a knife carefully around the edge of each custard. Invert onto a plate, and drizzle 1 teaspoon of coffee liqueur, if using, over each flan. Serve.

Gingerbread Snacking Cake

8 tablespoons (1 stick) unsalted
butter, room temperature, plus
more for pan

2½ cups all-purpose flour, plus more
for pan

2 teaspoons baking soda

2 teaspoons ground ginger

1½ teaspoons ground cinnamon

½ teaspoon ground cloves

½ teaspoon ground nutmeg

½ teaspoon salt

2 teaspoons baking powder

⅔ cup packed dark-brown sugar

1 cup unsulfured molasses

1 tablespoon freshly grated ginger

2 large eggs, room temperature,
lightly beaten
Confectioners' sugar, for dusting

Fresh ginger intensifies the spiciness of this cake, but if it is unavailable, increase the amount of ground ginger to 1 tablespoon.　　**serves 12**

1. Heat oven to 350°. Boil 1 cup water. Butter and flour a 9-by-13-inch cake pan; set aside. In a bowl, combine boiling water and baking soda; set aside. In a large bowl, sift together the flour, ground spices, salt, and baking powder, and set aside.

2. In an electric mixer fitted with the paddle attachment, cream the butter until light. Beat in the brown sugar until fluffy. Beat in the molasses, grated ginger, baking-soda mixture, and flour mixture. Beat in the eggs.

3. Pour the batter into the prepared pan; bake until a toothpick inserted in the center comes out clean, 30 to 35 minutes. Let cool on wire rack. Cut into squares, and dust with confectioners' sugar just before serving.

Maple Layer Cake

8 tablespoons (1 stick) unsalted
butter, room temperature, plus
more for pans

2¾ cups all-purpose flour, sifted,
plus more for pans

2 cups pure maple syrup

3 large eggs

1 tablespoon baking powder

¼ teaspoon salt

1 teaspoon ground ginger

1 cup milk

1 teaspoon pure vanilla extract

1½ cups (6 ounces) toasted walnuts,
chopped medium fine
Maple Buttercream Frosting
(recipe follows)

Each of these layers can also be eaten as a snacking cake, plain, or with just a crumble of maple sugar. Filled and frosted with Maple Buttercream Frosting, the cake can serve 16 people. **makes one 9-inch cake**

1. Heat oven to 350°. Butter two 9-by-2-inch-round cake pans, and dust them with flour. Tap out any excess flour, and set the pans aside.

2. In the bowl of an electric mixer fitted with the paddle attachment, beat the butter on medium speed, until creamy. Add the maple syrup, and beat until combined. Add the eggs, one at a time, beating thoroughly after each addition. Beat until combined.

3. In a large bowl, sift together the flour, baking powder, salt, and ginger. With the mixer on low speed, add the flour mixture to the butter mixture, and beat to combine. Beat in the milk and vanilla extract until combined. Then add ¾ cup toasted chopped walnuts, and, using a rubber spatula, stir until they are incorporated.

4. Divide the batter between the two prepared pans. Bake until golden and a cake tester inserted into the centers comes out clean, about 40 minutes; rotate the cake pans halfway through baking time to ensure even baking. Transfer pans to a wire rack to cool.

5. Turn out the cakes, and place one, top-side up, on a cake stand or platter. Spread 1½ cups maple-buttercream frosting evenly over the top. Place the second cake layer on top, and spread the remaining 2½ cups frosting around the sides and over the top. Using your hands, gently press the remaining ¾ cup walnuts onto the sides of the cake. Serve.

Maple Buttercream Frosting

6 large egg yolks

2 cups pure maple syrup

2 cups (4 sticks) unsalted
butter, chilled and cut into
small pieces

This frosting can be stored, refrigerated, in an airtight container up to two days. Before using, bring to room temperature, and beat with the whisk attachment of an electric mixer for several minutes to restore the fluffiness. **makes 4 cups**

1. Place the egg yolks in the bowl of an electric mixer fitted with the whisk attachment, and beat on high speed until light and fluffy, about 5 minutes.

2. Meanwhile, pour maple syrup into a medium saucepan, and place over medium-high heat; bring liquid to a boil. Cook until a candy thermometer registers 240° (soft-ball stage), about 15 minutes.

3. Remove the saucepan from the heat. While the electric mixer is running, pour the maple syrup in a slow, steady stream down the side of the bowl into the egg-yolk mixture (it is essential that the syrup touches the side of the bowl as you pour it in so the sugar will be very evenly incorporated and not splatter onto the sides of the bowl) until the syrup has been completely incorporated, about 1½ minutes. Beat until the bowl is just slightly warm to the touch, 5 to 6 minutes.

4. Add the butter, one piece at a time, until all of it has been completely incorporated and the frosting is fluffy, about 4 minutes more.

Sugar-dusted cubes of our Gingerbread Snacking Cake are perfect for a tea, a picnic, or on a casual stroll past the kitchen counter. Fresh and ground ginger, cloves, cinnamon, and nutmeg make this traditional treat soothing and, at the same time, spicy and stimulating.

Boston Cream Pie

FOR THE HOT-MILK SPONGE CAKE:

Unsalted butter for cake pan

1 cup sifted cake flour (not
self-rising), plus more for pan

¼ teaspoon salt

4 large eggs

1 cup sugar

¼ cup plus 2 tablespoons milk

1 vanilla bean, split

The lightness of this sponge cake comes from steadily whisking the sugar and eggs over hot water. Use a wire whisk or a handheld electric mixer. Prepare the cake and custard-cream several hours or even a day ahead, so they have sufficient time to cool and set.　　**makes one 9-inch cake**

TO MAKE THE CAKE:

1. Heat oven to 350°. Butter and flour a 9-by-2-inch-round cake pan. Line with parchment; set aside.

2. Sift together the cake flour and the salt. Sift again, two more times; set aside. In the bowl of an electric mixer fitted with the whisk attachment, mix the eggs and sugar until well combined. Place the bowl over a pot of gently simmering water; whisk until mixture is warm, about 110°, and the sugar is dissolved, about 6 minutes. Remove from heat; place bowl on mixer. Whisk the egg mixture on high speed until thickened and pale, about 6 minutes.

3. Meanwhile, in a small saucepan, combine the milk and vanilla bean. Place over medium heat until hot, being careful not to let boil. Remove and discard vanilla bean. With egg mixture beating, pour the hot milk into the egg mixture in a slow, steady stream. Turn off mixer. Transfer to a medium bowl; fold in the flour mixture. Pour into prepared pan.

4. Bake until the cake is golden brown and springs back when gently pressed, about 30 minutes. Transfer to a wire rack to cool for 15 minutes. Remove from pan, and cool completely.

FOR THE CUSTARD-CREAM FILLING:

6 large egg yolks

¾ cup sugar

6½ tablespoons cornstarch

⅛ teaspoon salt

3 cups milk

2 teaspoons pure vanilla extract

TO MAKE THE FILLING:

1. In a large bowl, whisk the egg yolks; set aside. In a medium saucepan, combine sugar, cornstarch, and salt. Gradually stir in the milk. Cook over medium heat, stirring constantly, until mixture thickens and begins to bubble, about 5 minutes. Remove from heat.

2. Slowly pour the hot milk mixture into the egg yolks while whisking. Return mixture to saucepan. Cook over medium heat, stirring constantly, until mixture begins to bubble, about 2 minutes. Remove from heat; stir in the vanilla extract.

3. Transfer filling to a medium bowl. Cover with plastic wrap, pressing wrap against the filling to prevent a skin from forming; chill in refrigerator until firm, at least 1 hour.

FOR THE SHINY CHOCOLATE GLAZE:

4 ounces best-quality semisweet
chocolate, coarsely chopped

½ cup heavy cream

TO MAKE THE GLAZE AND ASSEMBLE THE CAKE:

1. Split the cake into two layers; spread the bottom half with chilled filling. Place in the refrigerator to set, about 30 minutes. Wrap the remaining half of cake with plastic wrap; set aside.

2. In a medium-size heat-proof bowl, or the top of a double boiler, set over a pot of gently simmering water, combine the chocolate and the heavy cream. Stir occasionally until the chocolate melts, about 12 minutes. Remove from heat; set aside to cool for 10 minutes.

3. Remove cake from refrigerator; top with the reserved cake layer. Transfer cake to a serving plate; pour the chocolate glaze over the top. Allow to set 20 minutes before serving.

Not really a pie, but definitely creamy: Boston Cream Pie is a classic American cake. Two moist, light layers of sponge cake are filled with vanilla custard-cream and coated with a glistening chocolate glaze. It's not fancy, but it's as finely textured as any French pastry, and you can proudly present this on a pedestal cake stand.

Fresh-picked local strawberries are the heart, and a fresh-baked, all-butter biscuit is the soul, of a great strawberry shortcake. The biscuit's bottom half soaks up the lemon-tinged strawberry juices, and the top crowns a mound of vanilla whipped cream.

Strawberry Shortcake With Vanilla Whipped Cream

2 pints strawberries, hulled and halved

3 tablespoons freshly squeezed lemon juice

½ cup granulated sugar

2 cups all-purpose flour, plus more for dough

1 tablespoon baking powder

½ teaspoon salt

6 tablespoons cold unsalted butter, cut into small pieces

1 large whole egg

1½ cups plus 3 tablespoons heavy cream

1 large egg yolk

1 vanilla bean, split

1 tablespoon confectioners' sugar

For light, fluffy biscuits, handle the shortcake dough as little as possible.   **serves 4**

1. Heat oven to 375°. Place strawberries in a bowl; sprinkle with lemon juice and ¼ cup sugar. Let stand to release juices, about 1 hour. Meanwhile, in a large bowl, combine remaining ¼ cup sugar, flour, baking powder, and salt. Use a fork to cut in butter until mixture resembles coarse meal.

2. Whisk together the egg and ½ cup plus 2 tablespoons cream. Slowly add this mixture to the dry ingredients; mix with a fork until dough just comes together. Do not overmix. Transfer dough to a lightly floured surface; pat into a 6-inch square, 1 inch thick. Cut 4 rounds using a 2½-inch cookie cutter. Place on a parchment-lined baking sheet. Whisk together the egg yolk and 1 tablespoon cream; brush over tops of biscuits. Bake until golden brown, 25 to 30 minutes. Cool on wire racks for 15 minutes.

3. To make the vanilla whipped cream, place the remaining 1 cup cream and vanilla bean in a saucepan over medium heat; scald and remove from heat. Cover and steep for 10 minutes. Scrape seeds into cream, and discard pod. Pass the cream mixture through a fine strainer into a bowl set in a large bowl of ice and water. Let stand until completely cold. Transfer to a large chilled metal bowl; add confectioners' sugar. Whip by hand into soft peaks (an electric mixer will curdle the cream), about 5 minutes.

4. To assemble, slice the shortcakes open with a bread knife while warm. Divide strawberries and liquid among bottom halves of shortcakes; top with large dollops of the vanilla whipped cream and upper halves of shortcakes, and serve.

Summer Berry Cobbler

1½ pints blueberries

2 pints blackberries

½ cup plus 1 teaspoon sugar

2½ cups plus 2 tablespoons all-purpose flour

2 tablespoons freshly squeezed lemon juice

Dash of ground cinnamon

1 teaspoon salt

1 cup (2 sticks) cold unsalted butter, cut into small pieces

1 large egg yolk

1 tablespoon heavy cream

This cobbler encloses berries in a pâte brisée—classic French short-pastry dough.   **serves 8**

1. Heat oven to 400°. Place berries in a large bowl. Add ½ cup sugar, 2 tablespoons flour, the lemon juice, and the cinnamon. Toss to combine. Set aside.

2. To make the pâte brisée, place the remaining 2½ cups flour, 1 teaspoon sugar, and the salt in the bowl of a food processor, and process for a few seconds to combine. Add the butter; process until mixture resembles coarse meal, about 10 seconds. Add ¼ cup ice water in a slow, steady stream through the feed tube with the machine running, just until the dough holds together. Do not process for more than 30 seconds. Turn dough out onto a piece of plastic wrap. Press into a flattened circle, and wrap it in the plastic; refrigerate for at least 1 hour.

3. On a lightly floured surface, roll out the pastry into an 18-inch circle ⅛ inch thick. Fold the dough in half, and transfer to an 8½-by-2½-inch round gratin dish or deep-dish pie plate. Carefully press the dough into the bottom and sides of the dish, allowing the excess to hang over the edge.

4. Spoon the berry mixture into the prepared dish, and fold the pastry in over the fruit. Trim away excess pastry, leaving an opening of about 3 inches in the center. Chill cobbler in the refrigerator until dough is firm, 15 to 20 minutes.

5. Combine the egg yolk and cream in small bowl. Brush pastry with the egg wash. Place cobbler in oven. Bake until crust is golden, about 30 minutes. Reduce heat to 350°. Continue baking until juices start to bubble up over the crust, about 35 minutes more. Remove from oven, cool slightly, and serve.

A plate piled with our three favorite kinds of homemade cookies presents a pleasurable dilemma—which to eat first, Chocolate Chip, Peanut Butter, or Oatmeal Raisin? Any choice is a good one. All are thick and chewy, rich with butter and eggs, moist with two kinds of sugars, and will keep for up to a week. But only if there are any left.

Thick enough to hold up a candy-striped straw, a sweet and icy malted milk shake is a summer thriller, but our two-toned strawberry and vanilla shake is twice as nice as any you can buy. Blended in two batches, each with a whole pint of ice cream, the shakes fill soda-fountain tumblers in contrasting layers.

Gingersnap Raspberry Sandwiches

8 tablespoons (1 stick) unsalted butter, room temperature
¼ cup vegetable shortening
2 cups sugar
2 cups all-purpose flour
2 teaspoons baking soda
1 teaspoon ground cinnamon
1 tablespoon ground ginger
¼ cup pure maple syrup
1 large egg, beaten
1 cup raspberry jam with seeds

A bit of maple syrup gives our gingersnaps a rich flavor. Spicy and crisp by themselves, they are even better by the pair, with a layer of raspberry jam in the middle.   **makes 2 dozen**

1. Heat oven to 375° with one rack positioned in the center of the oven; line a baking sheet with parchment paper, and set aside.

2. In the bowl of an electric mixer fitted with the paddle attachment, cream butter, shortening, and 1 cup sugar on medium speed. In a large bowl, sift together the flour, baking soda, cinnamon, and ginger. Set aside.

3. Add the maple syrup to the butter mixture; beat to combine. Beat in the egg until well combined. Reduce mixer speed to low; slowly add the flour mixture, a little at a time, until well blended.

4. Place remaining cup sugar in a bowl. Measure 2 teaspoons dough; roll into a ball. Roll dough in sugar; transfer to sheet. Repeat, spacing balls 3 inches apart. Bake until golden, about 12 minutes. Transfer cookies to a wire rack to cool. Form and bake the remaining dough.

5. Spread about 2 teaspoons jam over the bottoms of half of the cookies; place a second cookie on top of jam-covered ones, making sandwiches. Serve.

Chocolate Chip Cookies

1 cup (2 sticks) unsalted butter, room temperature
1½ cups packed light-brown sugar
½ cup granulated sugar
1 teaspoon pure vanilla extract
1 large egg, room temperature
2 cups all-purpose flour
½ teaspoon baking soda
½ teaspoon salt
12 ounces semisweet chocolate, coarsely chopped, or one 12-ounce bag semisweet chocolate chips

You can substitute bittersweet chocolate for half of the semisweet chocolate.   **makes 2 dozen**

1. Heat oven to 375°. Line several baking sheets with parchment paper, and set aside.

2. Combine the butter and both sugars in the bowl of an electric mixer fitted with the paddle attachment, and beat until light and fluffy. Add the vanilla, and mix to combine. Add the egg, and continue beating until well combined.

3. In a medium bowl, whisk together the flour, baking soda, and salt. Slowly add the dry ingredients to the butter mixture. Mix on low speed until just combined. Stir in the chocolate chips.

4. Scoop out 2 tablespoons of dough, and place on a prepared baking sheet. Repeat with the remaining dough, placing scoops 3 inches apart. Bake for 16 to 18 minutes, or until just brown around the edges, rotating the pans between the oven shelves halfway through baking. Remove from the oven, and let cool slightly before removing the cookies from the baking sheets. Store in an airtight container at room temperature for up to 1 week.

Peanut Butter Cookies

8 tablespoons (1 stick) unsalted butter, room temperature
¾ cup smooth peanut butter
½ cup granulated sugar
½ cup packed dark-brown sugar
1 large egg
½ teaspoon pure vanilla extract
1 cup all-purpose flour
¾ teaspoon baking soda
Dry-roasted, salted peanuts, for sprinkling (optional)

These cookies can also be made with chunky peanut butter.   **makes 2 dozen**

1. Heat oven to 350°. Line several baking sheets with parchment paper, and set aside.

2. In the bowl of an electric mixer fitted with a paddle attachment, cream the butter, peanut butter, and both sugars together until light and fluffy. Add the egg and vanilla, and mix on medium speed until well combined.

3. In a medium mixing bowl, sift the flour and baking soda together. Add to the butter mixture, and beat just to combine.

4. Scoop out 2 tablespoons of dough, shape into a ball, and place on one of the prepared baking sheets. Repeat with the remaining dough, placing scoops 3 inches apart. Dip the tines of a fork in warm water; press the dough balls lightly with the back of the fork to flatten them slightly (dip the fork back in the water for each dough ball, to prevent sticking). Sprinkle with a few peanuts, if desired.

5. Transfer to the oven, and bake for 18 to 20 minutes, until golden brown, rotating the baking sheets between the oven shelves halfway through baking. Transfer baking sheets to a wire rack to cool. Store in an airtight container at room temperature up to 1 week.

Oatmeal Raisin Cookies

2 cups all-purpose flour
½ teaspoon salt
½ teaspoon ground cinnamon
1 teaspoon baking powder
1 teaspoon baking soda
1 cup (2 sticks) unsalted butter, room temperature
1 cup packed light-brown sugar
½ cup granulated sugar
1 tablespoon pure vanilla extract
3 tablespoons milk
2 large eggs
3 cups old-fashioned oats
1 cup raisins

Any dried fruit can be substituted for the raisins. Be sure the cookies are completely cool before storing in an airtight container.   **makes about 3 dozen**

1. In a medium bowl, whisk together flour, salt, cinnamon, baking powder, and baking soda. Set aside. In the bowl of an electric mixer fitted with the paddle attachment, combine the butter with both sugars, and beat until light and fluffy. Add vanilla, milk, and eggs, and mix well. Add the flour mixture, and beat until just combined. Remove bowl from the electric mixer, and stir in the oats and raisins. Place dough in the refrigerator until firm, about 2 hours or overnight.

2. Heat oven to 350°. Line several baking sheets with parchment paper, and set aside. Scoop out 2 tablespoons of dough, shape into a ball; place on one of the prepared sheets. Repeat with the remaining dough, spacing the dough 3 inches apart. Press down to flatten into 2-inch diameters.

3. Transfer to the oven, and bake until golden, but still soft in center, 16 to 18 minutes, rotating the pans between oven shelves halfway through baking. Remove from oven, and place on a wire rack to cool completely. Store in an airtight container at room temperature up to 1 week.

Brownies

12 tablespoons (1½ sticks) unsalted butter, cut in pieces, plus more for pan

8 ounces best-quality bittersweet or semisweet chocolate, such as Valrhona, roughly chopped

4 large eggs

1½ cups granulated sugar

½ cup packed dark-brown sugar

1 tablespoon pure vanilla extract

1⅓ cups sifted all-purpose flour

½ teaspoon salt

This recipe yields brownies that are moist and fudgy. If you prefer a lighter, cakier brownie, add an additional egg to the batter. **makes about twelve 3-inch squares**

1. Heat oven to 350°. Grease a 9-by-13-inch baking pan with butter, and set aside.

2. In the top of a double boiler or in a heat-proof bowl over simmering water, melt the butter and chocolate until smooth; stir occasionally. Remove from heat. Allow to cool to room temperature.

3. In a large mixing bowl, combine the eggs, granulated and brown sugars, and vanilla, and beat well with a wire whisk. In a separate bowl, combine the sifted flour and salt. Add the cooled chocolate mixture to the egg mixture and, using a wooden spoon, stir until well combined. Gradually add the flour mixture, and beat until thoroughly combined. Pour the batter into the prepared pan.

4. Bake until a tester inserted into the center of the brownie comes out clean, about 30 minutes. Do not overbake. Let stand on a rack in the pan until cool. Cut into 3-inch squares and serve. Store in an airtight container, at room temperature, up to 2 days.

Root Beer Float

1 pint vanilla ice cream

32 ounces root beer

There are many good-quality regional root beers. Buy the best one you can find in your area. **makes 4 drinks**

Scoop ½ cup ice cream into each of 4 tall glasses. Add enough root beer to fill each glass. Serve each with a long iced-tea spoon and straw.

Malted Milk Shakes

1 cup milk

6 tablespoons malted-milk powder, plus more for garnish

1 pint vanilla ice cream

1 pint chocolate or strawberry ice cream

Malted-milk balls for garnish (optional)

Malted milk shakes can be made with either chocolate or strawberry ice cream. Malted-milk powder, or Ovaltine, is available in most grocery stores. **makes 4**

1. Place ½ cup milk and 3 tablespoons malted-milk powder in the jar of a blender, and process until malt is dissolved. Add half the vanilla ice cream, and blend until smooth. With the motor running, add the remaining vanilla ice cream, 1 scoop at a time, until it is fully incorporated. Pour half the shake into a glass measuring cup, and place in freezer. Divide remaining half between two glasses, and place glasses in freezer. Allow to chill for 10 minutes before proceeding to step two.

2. Place remaining ½ cup milk and 3 tablespoons malt powder in clean jar of blender, and process until malt is dissolved. Add half the chocolate or strawberry ice cream, and blend until smooth. With motor running, add remaining ice cream, one scoop at a time, until fully incorporated. Divide half the shake between two empty glasses, and top off two partially filled glasses from freezer with remainder. Allow the half-filled glasses to freeze for 10 minutes. Stir reserved vanilla shake before topping off remaining glasses. Garnish with malted-milk powder and malted-milk balls if desired, and serve immediately.

Banana Split

½ cup heavy cream
½ vanilla bean, split
4 bananas, peeled, split lengthwise
4 scoops (½ pint) each of chocolate, coffee, and hazelnut ice cream
½ cup Chocolate Syrup (recipe below)
½ cup Caramel Sauce (recipe below)
  Wet Walnuts (recipe below)
  Fresh or brandied cherries

¾ cup sugar
¼ cup light corn syrup
4 ounces dark bittersweet chocolate, finely chopped
½ teaspoon pure vanilla extract

2 cups sugar
1½ cups heavy cream
2 tablespoons unsalted butter
1 teaspoon freshly squeezed lemon juice

1 cup walnut pieces
¼ cup maple syrup
¼ cup light corn syrup

Abundant choices make ice-cream sundaes a special sort of pleasure. You can add other ice-cream flavors, fruits, sauces, nuts, and candy garnishes, as well. Assemble all the ingredients, bowls, spoons, and scoops on a sideboard, and let everyone follow his or her heart's desire.   **makes 4**

1. Scrape the vanilla bean seeds into a medium bowl. Add the cream, and whip until soft peaks form.

2. Place 2 banana halves in each of four dishes. Top with 1 scoop each of chocolate, coffee, and hazelnut ice creams. Drizzle chocolate syrup and caramel sauce over the scoops of ice cream. Top with the vanilla whipped cream, wet walnuts, and cherries. Serve immediately.

Chocolate Syrup   **makes 1½ cups**

Combine the sugar, corn syrup and ¼ cup hot water in a saucepan; bring to a boil over medium-high heat. Reduce to a simmer; cook until the sugar is dissolved, about 1 minute. Remove from the heat, and stir in chocolate until smooth. Stir in the vanilla and ¼ cup warm water. Serve (or store in an airtight container, refrigerated, up to 1 week; warm before serving).

Caramel Sauce   **makes 2½ cups**

Place sugar and ½ cup water in a saucepan; stir. Cook, without stirring, over medium heat until boiling. Occasionally wipe down sides of pan with a wet pastry brush to prevent stray granules of sugar from crystallizing. When sugar just begins to brown, swirl pan to help dissolve the sugar; cook until sugar is a rich amber color. Reduce heat to low; gradually add the cream while stirring with a wooden spoon. Add butter and lemon juice, and stir to combine. Serve (or store in an airtight container, refrigerated, up to 1 week, and warm before serving).

Wet Walnuts   **makes 1 cup**

Heat oven to 350°. Place walnuts in a baking pan in a single layer; toast until golden brown and fragrant, about 10 minutes. Remove pan from the oven, and set aside. Combine the maple syrup, corn syrup, and walnuts in a bowl, and stir until nuts are well coated. Serve (or store, refrigerated in an airtight container, up to 1 week).

Root Beer Floats are one of
Martha's favorite fountain treats.
She makes them the traditional
way, stacking generous scoops of
hard-packed vanilla ice cream
in a tall glass and pouring the
best-quality root beer to the rim.

A footed glass sundae boat—
Titanic-size preferred—is the
best dish for a Banana Split.
Ours is a colossal combination
of favorite dessert flavors;
chocolate, coffee, and hazelnut
ice creams and homemade
caramel sauce and chocolate
syrup. There's also real vanilla in
the whipped cream and pure
maple syrup coating the walnuts.
And there should be a bite of
banana in every spoonful, too!

the guide

Items pictured but not listed are from private collections. Addresses and telephone numbers of sources may change prior to or following publication, as may price and availability of any item.

front cover
Martha's sweater *by Cashmere Cashmere.* **Jeans** *by Levi's.* **Angora socks** *by Hue.* **Wardrobe** *by Nicole Di Miceli.* **Hair and makeup** *by Eva Screevo.*

Long Mornings

page 15
Soy flakes, $2.29 per pound, *from Whole Foods, 2421 Broadway, New York, NY 10024; 212-874-4000, or local health food stores,* and **wheat flakes,** $1.03 per 1-pound bag, *from Macrobiotic Company of America, 799 Old Leicester Highway, Asheville, NC 28806; 800-643-8909.*

page 16
Wheat berries, $1.49 per 2-pound bag, and **yellow millet,** $1.20 per 1-pound bag, *from Macrobiotic Company of America, see above.*

page 18
Kitchen glasses, $12 for set of six (DJG001), *from Martha By Mail, 800-950-7130; www.marthabymail.com.*

pages 20 and 21
Master-Chef **nonstick fry pan,** $80, *from All-Clad, 800-255-2523.*

page 28
Le Creuset 10 1/2-inch square **griddle,** $64.95 (#15528), *from Sur La Table, 1765 Sixth Avenue, Seattle, WA 98134; 800-243-0852.*

pages 30 and 31
Luna **salad plate** (in Ocean), *from the Calvin Klein Home Collection, 800-294-7978 for nearest retailer, or from Bloomingdale's, 212-705-2000; www.bloomingdales.com.* **Deep-frying thermometer,** $13.75, 14-inch pastry bag, $3.25, #4 star tip, $1.25, *from Broadway Panhandler, 477 Broome Street, New York, NY 10013; 212-966-3434; www.broadwaypanhandler.com.*

page 32
Belgian waffler, $49.95, *from Broadway Panhandler, see above.*

Home for Lunch

page 38
Hotel-silver dinner plate, *from Rooms & Gardens, 290 Lafayette Street, New York, NY 10012; 212-431-1297.* **Shiitake mushrooms,** $15 per pound, **oyster mushrooms,** $13 per pound, and **cremini mushrooms,** $6 per pound, *from Dean & DeLuca, 560 Broadway, New York, NY 10012; 212-431-1691 or 800-999-0306; www.dean-deluca.com.*

page 44
Thick-cut bacon, $5.99 per 1-pound package, *from Balducci's, 424 Sixth Avenue, New York, NY 10011; 212-673-2600 or 800-225-3822; www.balducci.com.*

page 45
Fingerling potatoes, from Indian Rock Produce, 530 California Road, Quakertown, PA 18951; 800-882-0512. **Quahog clams,** 30 cents each, *from Wellfleet Oyster and Clam Company, P.O. Box 1439, Lewis Paine Way, Wellfleet, MA 02667; 800-572-9227 or 508-349-2717.* Or shucked clams, $7.99 per dozen, *from Citarella, 2135 Broadway, New York, NY 10023; 212-874-0383.*

page 47
Marble-topped bistro table, $2,000, *from Rooms & Gardens, see above.*

page 54
Spicy fruit chutney, $7 per 12-ounce jar, *from Dean & DeLuca, see above.*

page 55
Madras **curry powder,** $6 for 4 ounces, *from Adriana's Caravan, 800-316-0820. Mail order only.*

What to Have for Dinner

page 61
Keyaki tray, $125, and **brown Pashmina shawl,** starting at $315, *from Ad Hoc Softwares, 410 West Broadway, New York, NY 10012; 212-925-2652.*

pages 63 and 64
San Marzano plum tomatoes, $3.75 per 28-ounce can, *from Dean & DeLuca, 560 Broadway, New York, NY 10012; 212-431-1691 or 800-999-0306; www.dean-deluca.com.* **Food mill,** $35, *from Bridge Kitchenware, 214 East 52nd Street, New York, NY 10022; 212-838-1901 or 800-274-3435; www.bridgekitchenware.com.*

Victor Guedes extra-virgin olive oil, $13.50 per 750-ml bottle; and **Victor Guedes pure olive oil,** $12 per one-quart can, *both from O Padeiro, 641 Sixth Avenue, New York, NY 10011; 212-414-9661.* **Olive oil** (KEV001) $18 per 34-ounce bottle *from Martha By Mail; 800-950-7130 or www.marthabymail.com.*

page 66
16-inch round pizza stone, $29.95, **14-by-24-inch pizza peel,** $15.25, and **Oxo 4-inch round pizza wheel,** $10.95, *from Broadway Panhandler, 477 Broome Street, New York, NY 10013; 212-966-3434; www.broadwaypanhandler.com.*

page 72
Round grill pan, $27.95, *from Bridge Kitchenware, see above.*

page 74
Instant-read thermometer, $11.90, *from Bridge Kitchenware, see above.*

pages 76 and 77
15-by-12-by-2-inch stainless-steel roasting pan, $38, and 1 1/2-cup **fat separator,** $6, *from Dean & DeLuca, see above.*

Food for Gatherings

page 80
Print *by Maria Robledo, 212-406-3211.* **White frame,** *from Sky Frame, 96 Spring Street, New York, NY 10012; 212-925-7856.* **Martha Stewart Everyday Colors,** in "Caneware" (H09), *available from Kmart (800-866-0086 for store locations), and in Sears mall stores (800-972-4687 for store locations).*

page 83
Cipollini onions, *from Indian Rock Produce, 530 California Road, Quakertown, PA 18951; 800-882-0512.* **Guajillo chiles,** $3.15 for 2 ounces, *from Kitchen Market, 218 Eighth Avenue, New York, NY 10011; 212-243-4433.*

page 90
French Charles X painted console table with marble top, $8,300, *from Rooms & Gardens, 290 Lafayette Street, New York, NY 10012; 212-431-1297.*

Sides and Small Suppers

page 96
10-inch tin-lined brass-handled gratin dish, $78, *from Bridge Kitchenware, 214 East 52nd*

Street, New York, NY 10022; 212-838-6746 or 800-274-3435; or www.bridgekitchenware.com.

page 106
Stainless-steel potato ricer, $37.50, from Bridge Kitchenware, see above.

page 110
Parmigiano-Reggiano, $11.99 per pound, from Murray's Cheese Shop, 257 Bleecker Street, New York, NY 10014; 212-243-3289, and $19.75 per pound, from Zingerman's Delicatessen, 888-636-8162.

Sweet Endings

page 118
Louis XVI celadon dessert plate, $28, by Jean-Paul Pichon from Intérieurs, 114 Wooster Street, New York, NY 10012; 212-343-0800.

page 131
Antique garden chair, $200, from Rooms & Gardens, 290 Lafayette Street, New York, NY 10012; 212-431-1297.

page 136
Valrhona chocolate, $15 per pound, from Dean & DeLuca, 560 Broadway, New York, NY 10012; 212-431-1691 or 800-999-0306; www.dean-deluca.com.

page 137
Brandied cherries, $21 per 500-gram jar, from Dean & DeLuca, see above.

page 139
Vintage painted **tole tray**, $150, from David Stypmann Co., 190 Sixth Avenue, New York, NY 10013; 212-226-5717.

page 140
8-inch transferware plate, $35, from the Tomato Factory, 2 Somerset Street, Hopewell, NJ, 08525; 609-466-9833.

If you have enjoyed this book, please join us as a subscriber to MARTHA STEWART LIVING *magazine. The annual subscription rate is $26 for ten issues. Call toll-free 800-999-6515, or visit our web site, www.marthastewart.com.*

Other books available in The Best of Martha Stewart Living series:

ARRANGING FLOWERS

CRAFTS AND KEEPSAKES FOR THE HOLIDAYS
(Christmas with Martha Stewart Living, Volume 3)

DECORATING FOR THE HOLIDAYS
(Christmas with Martha Stewart Living, Volume 2)

DECORATING DETAILS

DESSERTS

GREAT PARTIES

CHRISTMAS WITH MARTHA STEWART LIVING
(Volume 1)

GOOD THINGS

GREAT AMERICAN WREATHS

HOW TO DECORATE

HANDMADE CHRISTMAS

WHAT TO HAVE FOR DINNER

SPECIAL OCCASIONS

HOLIDAYS

contributors

A special thanks to Susan Spungen and the food department at Martha Stewart Living, and to the many photographers, art directors, editors, and stylists whose inspiration and ideas contributed to this volume, notably Stephana Bottom, Stephen Drucker, Beth Eakin, Jennifer Herman, Jim McKeever, Melissa Morgan, Ayesha Patel, Eric A. Pike, Debra Puchalla, Scot Schy, Duane Stapp, and Gael Towey. Thanks also to the entire staff of Martha Stewart Living Omnimedia and to everyone at Oxmoor House, Clarkson Potter, Satellite Graphics, and Quebecor Printing whose work and dedication helped produce this book. Finally, thank you to Martha, for instilling in us a love of good food.

Photography

William Abranowicz
pages 8, 51, 89 (inset), 109, front cover

Quentin Bacon
pages 68, 69

Christopher Baker
pages 126, 127

Beatriz da Costa
pages 12, 13, 14, 18, 19, 23, 36, 37, 42, 51 (inset), 53, 55, 57, 67, 83, 94, 110, 111, 129, 132, 134

Reed Davis
pages 26, 28, 29, 58, 62, 64, 65, 76, 77, 79, 106, 107, 118

Dana Gallagher
pages 30, 31, 41, 70, 71, 96

Gentl & Hyers
pages 10, 85, 93

Lisa Hubbard
page 2

Stephen Lewis
page 116

Maura McEvoy
pages 48, 52, 103 (inset)

James Merrell
pages 5, 45, 138

Amy Neunsinger
page 104

Victoria Pearson
pages 17, 40, 43, 97, 101, 105

Maria Robledo
pages 3, 4, 34, 39, 44, 46, 73 (inset), 80, 84, 86, 87, 89, 90, 98, 114, 118 (inset), 121, 122, 130, 131, back cover

David Sawyer
pages 60, 61

Ann Stratton
pages 82, 99, 123

Petrina Tinslay
page 73

Simon Watson
pages 20, 21, 24, 103, 117

Jonelle Weaver
page 124

Anna Williams
pages 32, 33, 74, 75, 112, 113, 120, 133, 139

index